Classic Finishing Techniques

Classic Finishing Techniques

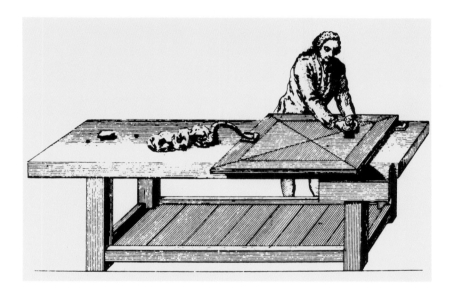

Sam Allen

 STERLING PUBLISHING CO., INC. NEW YORK

Acknowledgments

M Y THANKS GO to the following people, companies, and institutions for their help with the research for this book: Virginia Allen, Wayne Ruth, Mark Johnson, Grand County Library, Utah State Library, Ohio University Library, Smithsonian Institution Library, A. F. Suter & Co., Ltd. (Swan Wharf, London, England), William Zinsser & Co., Inc. (Somerset, New Jersey).

Library of Congress Cataloging-in-Publication Data

Allen, Sam.
   Classic finishing techniques / Sam Allen.
      p.   cm.
   Includes bibliographical references and index.
   ISBN 0-8069-0512-3
   1. Wood finishing.   2. Polishes.   I. Title.
TT325.A43   1994
684.1'043—dc20

94-16844
CIP

10 9 8 7 6 5 4 3 2 1

Published by Sterling Publishing Company, Inc.
387 Park Avenue South, New York, N.Y. 10016
© 1994 by Sam Allen
Distributed in Canada by Sterling Publishing
c/o Canadian Manda Group, One Atlantic Avenue, Suite 105
Toronto, Ontario, Canada M6K 3E7
Distributed in Great Britain and Europe by Cassell PLC
Villiers House, 41/47 Strand, London, WC2N 5JE, England
Distributed in Australia by Capricorn Link (Australia) Pty Ltd.
P.O. Box 6651, Baulkham Hills, Business Centre, NSW 2153, Australia
Printed and Bound in Hong Kong
All rights reserved

Sterling ISBN 0-8069-0512-3

Contents

Introduction

ANYONE WHO APPRECIATES fine antique furniture has probably noticed that the original finishes used on antiques have a unique beauty. When you build an antique reproduction, you may find it hard to duplicate the look of the original finish using modern products. The best way to achieve the desired look is to use authentic finishing materials and techniques appropriate to the time period of the antique. This book is devoted solely to these materials that I call classic finishes.

Classic finishes are like fine China; they can be very beautiful and last for many years if properly cared for, but, like fine China, they can be easily damaged if they are not treated correctly. Many modern finishes are like plastic dinnerware. They look good and will stand up to heavy abuse, but they lack the delicate quality of the more fragile classic finish. In most cases, classic finishes require more expertise to apply than their modern counterparts. Applying a classic finish is more of an art than a science. The results can be unpredictable, and it is often necessary to experiment on a similar piece of wood before applying the finish to the project.

Classic finishes are not perfect; if they were, there would have been no incentive to develop the modern finishes used today. Each finish has advantages and disadvantages. You must weigh the advantages against the disadvantages and determine for yourself whether or not to use a classic finish.

This book is intended for wood finishers who have had experience with modern finishes and are familiar with basic finishing procedures and are now ready to move into more advanced finishing techniques. If you are just getting started in wood finishing, I recommend my book *Finishing Basics*. If you are looking for a book about intermediate and advanced techniques using modern finishing products, I recommend my book *Wood Finisher's Handbook*.

Chapter One of this book gives an overview of the materials and techniques that I call classic finishes; these include French polish, varnish, oil, wax, natural stains, chemical stains, fumed finishes, and milk paint. Chapter Two covers preparing wood for a classic finish.

The French-polish finish is one of the most useful and popular of the classic finishes, so I have devoted Chapters Three–Six to various aspects of the French-polishing process. Chapter Three describes the various supplies used in French polishing. The application of a standard French-polish finish is covered in Chapter Four. There are several variations on the standard French-polishing process that are used for special applications; these are discussed in Chapter Five. Defects can occur in a French polish during application or as a result of age or abuse; correcting these defects is the subject of Chapter Six.

The remainder of the book covers other types of classic finishing products and their application. Chapter Seven examines varnishes. Chapter Eight is a discussion of oil finishes. Wax finishes are covered in Chapter Nine. Stains, which have either dyes or pigments, change the color of the wood; classic-type stains are explored in Chapter Ten.

Chemical stains react with natural substances in the wood to produce a color change; different chemicals have various effects on wood. One of the most popular chemical stains is the fumed finish. Fumed finishes use ammonia fumes to change the color of the wood. They are most closely associated with oak furniture. Chapter Eleven discusses how to use fumed finishes and other chemical stains. Many antiques are finished with paint. Chapter Twelve is about one authentic type of paint finish, milk paint.

Old-time finishers subjected themselves to hazards that we would consider unacceptable today, so I have modified some of the techniques, and I recommend that you always wear plastic gloves while you work. Use adequate ventilation to avoid getting sick from the fumes, and wear eye protection when there is a chance that the finishing products can splash in your eyes. I have included some of the old recipes that include hazardous chemicals, for historical interest. If you decide to use any of them, you do it at your own risk. Be sure you know how to handle the materials, and use the proper safety precautions that I have described in the appropriate sections.

Sam Allen

Types of Classic Finish

CHOOSING WHICH CLASSIC finish to use is a matter of personal preference. You may choose to use one of the finishes on a piece of furniture simply because you like the look it produces, even if it is not historically accurate. Classic finishes can even be used on modern furniture with beautiful results. If you want to be completely accurate when making an antique reproduction, then you should only use finishing materials that were in use at the time the original antique was made. In this chapter, I will give you a historical overview of the finishing process and briefly describe the various classic finishes to help you decide which finish to use on a particular project.

Soon after modern products were introduced into widespread use early in the 20th century, much of the traditional way of wood finishing was forgotten. Much of what we know today comes from a few old books that were written on the subject (Illus. 1-1). Some of the most useful of these old books include: *A Treatise of Japaning and Varnishing* (John Stalker and George Parker, Oxford, 1688), (*L'Art du Menuisier en Meubles*) *The Art of the Woodworker* (André Jacques Roubo, Paris, 1769), *The Cabinet Dictionary* (Thomas Sheraton, London, 1803), *The Cabinet-Maker's Guide . . .* (Ansel Phelps publisher, Greenfield, Massachusetts, 1825), and *Encyclopedia of Practical Receipts and Processes* (William Dick, New York, 1875). Since references in these books can be vague and sometimes rely on the reader already having some knowledge of the procedures discussed, modern research must also include examination of antiques and experimentation with the old materials. The procedures described in this book are based on my own experience with the materials described.

Woodworking and wood finishing are such ancient crafts that their origins are not known. Some of the earliest surviving examples of woodwork are found in Egyptian tombs dating from 4000 BC. These examples show a fully developed woodworking tradition, so we can assume that the craft was developed much earlier. The wood-finishing materials used in these early times were natural waxes, resins, and oils. These same materials have remained popular to this very day.

In the following pages, I will cover finishing techniques dating from the mid-1600's to the mid-1900's. This time

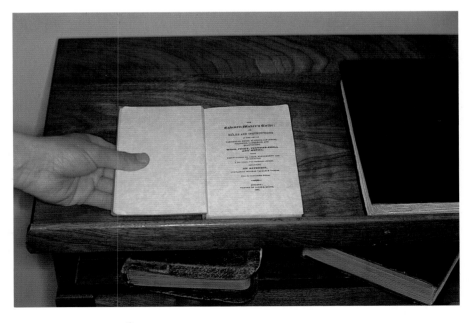

Illus. 1-1. Many classic finishing techniques might have been lost forever if they had not been recorded in a few rare old books. The finishes I describe are based on old formulas from these books and my own observations of old finishes and experimentation with the ingredients used to create them.

range can be broken into two periods, the period from the 1600's to approximately 1830 and the period from approximately 1830 to approximately 1940.

From 1688, when A *Treatise of Japaning and Varnishing*, by John Stalker and George Parker, was published, to 1825, when *The Cabinet-Maker's Guide . . .* was published, the same basic materials and techniques were known and used. The materials and methods described in *The Cabinet-Maker's Guide . . .* are very similar to those described by John Stalker and George Parker over 130 years earlier. However, during the period in which *The Cabinet-Maker's Guide* was written, some finishes were more widely used and others less widely used than at other times. Shellac is a good example. Stalker and Parker give a lot of information about shellac (and "seed-lacc") in their book, but it appears from other evidence that shellac and seed-lacc were not widely used until many years later.

Geography also plays a role in what finishes were used during these time periods. Even when shellac was used regularly in Europe, it was uncommon in America, probably because it was too expensive. The shellac would be taxed once when it was imported from India to England, and a second tax would be added when it was exported to America. In isolated areas such as the American Southwest, even the most basic raw ingredients would be too expensive when all of the freight charges were added up; so very simple finishes using native materials such as beeswax persisted in these areas long after other finishes were being used in other parts of the world.

Prior to the Renaissance, European wood finishes were very simple. Usually a natural oil such as walnut oil or linseed oil was applied to protect the wood, or the wood was rubbed with beeswax. After the Renaissance, a higher degree of finish was applied to fine furniture. In many cases, the same two materials, linseed oil and beeswax, were used but they were applied in a way to bring them to a higher degree of polish. In his book *The Art of the Woodworker*, André Jacques Roubo describes a method of applying beeswax that produces a high-gloss finish.

By the 1600's, varnishes were used on some pieces of furniture. Spirit varnishes that used alcohol as the solvent for natural resins such as sandarac and mastic combined with smaller quantities of other resins were used for the best work because they could be made colorless (white). When more durability and water resistance was needed, the darker oil varnishes were used. Oil varnishes were made by combining linseed oil or other oils with various resins.

Stains used to change the color of wood have been known for centuries, but they were not commonly used until the 1700's, when bright red and black stains were fashionable. During the period from 1688 to 1830, stains were mostly made from natural plant dyes or chemicals that altered the natural color of the wood.

Around 1830, things began to change in the finishing industry. Some new raw ingredients were discovered and new manufacturing techniques developed. In the period from 1830 to 1940, shellac became one of the dominant products. New oil-based varnishes were also developed that used kauri resin, a superior type of copal that was imported from New Zealand. The use of tung oil became more prevalent when tung tree farms were planted in Florida during the 1920's. Around the 1860's aniline dyes were developed. This led to the use of reliable stains available in a wide range of colors. The aniline dyes could be formulated to dissolve in alcohol, water, or oil.

Modern synthetic finishing materials started to become available as early as 1909 with the development of phenolics. Nitrocellulose lacquer was invented in 1855, but it didn't come into widespread use until after World War I. Alkyd resins were developed in the 1920's. Vinyl resins came into use in the late 1930's. In the 1940's, urethane resins were being produced and the other synthetics were gaining acceptance; this marks the end of what I call the classic period of wood finishing.

FRENCH POLISH

The French-polish finish uses spirit varnish applied with a cloth pad. Some early recipes for French polish used mastic and sandarac in combination with other resins. The lac resin has been known for centuries in India and surrounding areas, but it wasn't widely known in Europe until the late 1600's.

By the time French polishing reached the height of its popularity in the late 1800's, shellac was the main ingredient in French polish. At first it was applied as a spirit varnish with a brush. The method of applying spirit varnish with a pad was developed in France sometime before 1800.

In *A Treatise of Japaning and Varnishing*, first published in 1688, Stalker and Parker may have been referring to French polishers in their book when they talk about varnish *dawbers*; this would put the development of French polishing earlier than 1688. Even though the process may have been introduced to England at this early date, it was not widely accepted. Stalker and Parker's remarks about varnish dawbers are not favorable.

Around 1815, the French-polishing process of applying

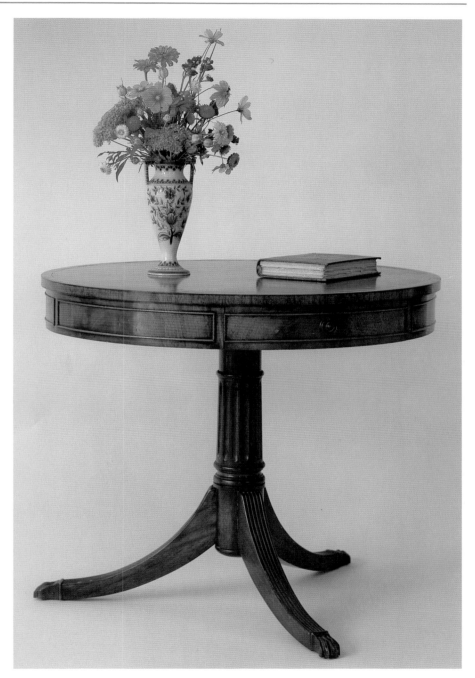

Illus. 1-2. A French-polish finish adds the final touch of elegance to a classic piece of furniture.

the shellac with a pad became widely used. The process evolved into two slightly different methods in France and Great Britain. In this book, I will describe both the French and the British methods.

Despite the fact that the French polish is one of the newest of the classic finishes, it is probably the most important one. A French-polish finish has a delicate beauty that is hard to achieve through any other process (Illus. 1-2).

Even though furniture made earlier than 1800 probably wasn't originally finished with French polish, most surviving pieces have been French-polished at a later date. The look of the French-polish finish has now become closely associated with fine antiques; so unless you are striving for complete historical accuracy, the French-polish finish is appropriate for most antique reproductions that require a fine finish.

VARNISHES

The term varnish has had several meanings over the years. There are generally two types of varnishes. *Spirit varnishes* use alcohol as the solvent. Natural resins that dissolve in alcohol are mixed together to form the varnish. *Oil varnish* is composed of various natural oils and resins.

Varnish is a good choice when durability is important. For example, chairs are often varnished (Illus. 1-3).

Certain types of varnish produce a very hard film; this property makes it possible to rub the surface with fine abrasives to produce effects ranging from a satin sheen to a high gloss.

OIL FINISHES

Natural vegetable oils have been used for wood finishing for centuries. The most commonly used oil is linseed oil. It is pressed from the seed of the flax (linen) plant. Other oils such as walnut, poppyseed, and tung oil are also important in wood finishing.

Oil finishes are easy to apply and bring out the natural beauty of the wood. They don't form a surface film, so the natural texture of the wood is apparent. An oil finish is historically accurate for any project ranging from contemporary pieces to those that date back to the earliest examples of woodworking. "Country" pieces were likely to have an oil finish since other types of finishing materials were unavailable, too expensive, or too difficult to apply for the rural craftsman (Illus. 1-4). Before the introduction of French-polishing methods, many of the finest pieces of

Illus. 1-3. Traditional varnish was used on this reproduction Shaker rocker.

Illus. 1-4. This Shaker jelly cupboard reproduction was finished with the oil and beeswax finish described in Chapter Eight.

Illus. 1-5. Wax has been used for centuries as a wood finish. This illustration from Roubo's *The Art of the Woodworker* shows wax being applied to a veneered panel.

furniture were given an oil finish. Today we associate an oil finish with a dull or satin sheen, but it is possible to produce a high gloss when many coats are used and the finish is rubbed vigorously.

WAX FINISHES

Wax is another finishing product that goes back to the earliest beginnings of woodworking. Beeswax is the type of wax that has been used most commonly throughout most of the history of woodworking (Illus. 1-5). Other natural waxes have been added to the list of available finishing materials since the 1700's, so that now there are many to choose from. Wax can be used as a stand-alone finish or as a final protective coating on top of another finishing product. Wax gives the wood a very mellow look.

STAINS

Stains are dyes or pigments used to color wood. In the past many natural substances were used as stains. These vegetable stains are derived from plants and trees (Illus. 1-6). Some of these stains fade after long exposure to light, so the color we see on antiques today is often very different from the original color. During the 1700's, bright red, yellow, and black stains were favored. Over the years these stains have faded to the warm browns we now associate with these antique pieces. If you can examine an area that has been protected from the light, under a drawer pull, for example, you may still see a bright red stain.

Today, there are two options when staining an antique reproduction. You can use a stain that reproduces the faded color and look of age seen on the originals, or you can use the original types of stains and duplicate the original finish as it appeared when the piece was new. One of the advantages of using the original materials is that if you can wait long enough, eventually the finish will age to look just like the original finish.

CHEMICAL STAINS AND FUMED FINISHES

Chemicals can be used to change the color of wood. Chemical stains have been used for centuries. One of the

Illus. 1-6. Walnut husks are one of several natural substances that are used to make vegetable stains.

main advantages of a chemical stain is that you can use it to alter the natural coloring material in the wood instead of adding a dye or pigment. A chemical stain will enhance the natural grain pattern and color variations instead of hiding them. The major disadvantages of chemical stains are that they consist of strong chemicals that can be dangerous and the results vary from one piece of wood to another.

The fumed finish is one of the most popular chemical stains. Wood that has a high tannin content, particularly oak, can be colored by the fuming process. This process uses ammonia fumes to chemically alter the color of the wood. Because this change doesn't involve the addition of a stain, the color doesn't obscure the grain.

Fumed oak furniture was very popular in the 1920's and 1930's. If you have ever tried to duplicate the color of a piece of old oak furniture, you have probably found that modern stains can't produce the same effect. Fumed oak was often protected with dark wax.

MILK PAINT

Paint has been found on early Egyptian furniture. It has been used constantly ever since. There have been various types of paint used. Milk paint is one type that is of ancient origin. It is useful today when you want to give an antique reproduction an authentic-looking paint finish (Illus. 1-7).

You can purchase commercially made milk paint in powdered form. This makes it easy to produce an authentic color, because the manufacturer uses authentic types of pigments. Some of these pigments will fade or change color with age just as they did on the original pieces, so after a few years the modern milk paint will be hard to tell from paint applied a hundred years ago.

SAMPLE CASE

A sample case (Illus. 1-8) is useful when you are working with classic finishes. These finishes will have different effects on different types of wood. It is a good idea to experiment first on small samples of the wood before you commit to using the finish on a large project. Instead of just using any old scrap of wood, make some uniformly sized samples of the woods you will be using; then you can save your samples for future reference. Write down

Illus. 1-7. Milk paint makes an authentic-looking finish for this Windsor chair. Intentional distressing on high-wear areas such as the front legs and the seat gives the chair an antique look.

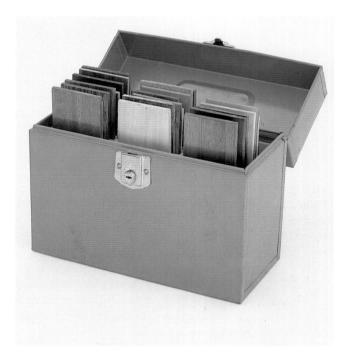

Illus. 1-8. Make a case in which to keep your samples of different finishes. These samples are useful when you are trying to decide on the type of finish to use on a piece of furniture.

the finishing steps you used on the back of the sample in pen. When you are planning a project, you can look through your samples to find the finish that you like best.

The surface of the sample must be prepared just the same as you will be preparing the final project. If you test a stain on a rough board, it will appear much darker than it will when you apply it to a smoothed one.

NECESSARY EQUIPMENT

To prepare some of the materials described in this book, you will need some special equipment. A scale is needed to weigh the materials. The scale can be a simple postal scale or a balance type of scale.

A mortar and pestle are necessary if you will be working with raw resins or dyestuffs (raw materials for dyes). They may need to be bruised, broken, or ground to powder for various purposes. The mortar and pestle don't have to be very large; in fact, if you will only be making small quantities, a small mortar and pestle is an advantage. Stores that sell specialty cooking tools will probably have a small mortar and pestle.

To measure fluids, use a graduated flask like the ones chemists use or ordinary measuring cups. Use glass measuring cups because plastic may be melted by some of the ingredients, and metal can react with some ingredients to form compounds that will discolor the wood.

Here is a list of items based on a list in Stalker and Parker's book that may prove as useful today as they did in 1688:

1. Two strainers made of fine flannel or coarse linen, shaped like a funnel. One is used for straining white varnish, the other for lac-varnish.
2. Two funnels: one for lac-varnish, the other for white varnish.
3. Several glass bottles to store varnish and several gally pots to hold the varnish as you apply it.
4. Several varnishing tools or small pencils (brushes).
5. Mussel shells to mix colors in.
6. Dutch rushes to smooth the work.
7. Tripoli abrasive to polish your work.
8. Linen rags.
9. Materials used for cleanup.

Illus. 1-9. In 1688, Stalker and Parker recommended using seashells as containers to hold ingredients as you are preparing them. They also recommended having a variety of glass and earthenware containers on hand to store finishing materials. It is still a good idea to use glass or earthenware containers when using classic finishing materials, because the solvents may dissolve plastic and metal containers and cause discoloration.

CHAPTER TWO

Preparing Wood for a Classic Finish

MOST CLASSIC FINISHES will emphasize small defects in the wood's surface, so a smooth surface is very important. Sandpaper or other abrasive products have been around for a long time, but until recently they were only used for the final steps of smoothing the wood. The majority of the surface preparation work was done with planes and scrapers. You can use modern power sanders to prepare the surface for a classic finish, but for historical accuracy and the best possible finish, I recommend that you use planes and scrapers, followed with a small amount of hand-sanding when necessary (Illus. 2-1).

PLANES

Planes smooth the wood by shearing off a thin slice of the surface (Illus. 2-2). The sole of the plane rides over humps and valleys in the surface, so the resulting surface is flatter than the previous one. If you are interested in a complete discussion on the use and care of planes, I recommend my book *Plane Basics*. In this chapter, I will cover the most important aspects of using planes to smooth the surface of a board in preparation for a classic finish.

When you build a project, you can either use mill-surfaced lumber or start with rough lumber and surface it entirely with planes. The important step for classic fin-

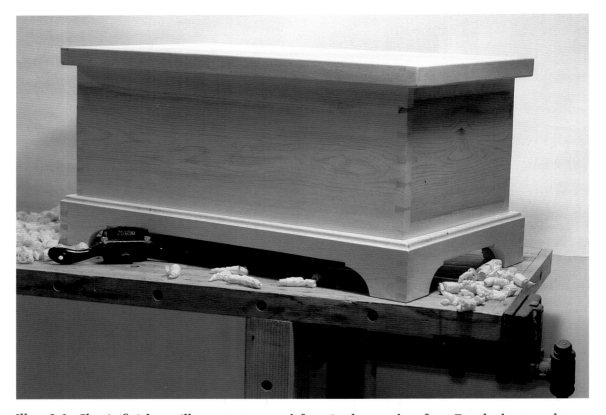

Illus. 2-1. Classic finishes will accentuate any defects in the wood surface. For the best results, make the surface as smooth as possible. This chest has been planed with hand planes and smoothed with a scraper.

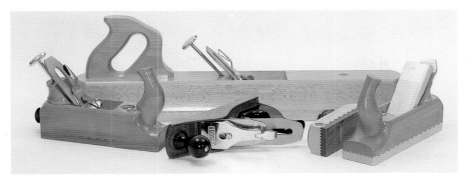

Illus. 2-2. Hand planes will smooth the surface of the board without leaving modern tool marks. When you are striving for complete authenticity on an antique reproduction, I recommend that you use hand planes to surface the wood.

ishing is the final smoothing with a smooth plane. Mill-surfaced lumber will have mill marks left by the planer. These marks are often very small ripples that are hardly noticeable on the bare lumber, but after you have applied a French polish they will stand out prominently. Mill marks often persist even after sanding because the sandpaper tends to conform to the surface. A light planing with a hand plane will remove the mill marks (Illus. 2-3).

If you are using planes to surface rough lumber, the initial steps are done using planes with a slight curvature to the cutting edge called a *camber*. This camber makes the plane cut better when you are taking deep roughing cuts. The cambered cutting edge will leave ripples on the surface of the board. The final step in surfacing the board is to remove these marks with a smooth plane.

A smooth plane is a short plane about 9 to 10 inches long. Smooth planes are available in both metallic and wooden types. Both types produce good results. I favor

the wooden plane because it seems that its wooden sole rides more easily over the board and slightly polishes the wood surface. The smooth plane has an iron that is ground straight with no camber.

Sharpening a Smooth Plane Iron

Before using a smooth plane to smooth the surface of a board, make sure that it is sharpened correctly. An important step in sharpening that is often neglected is to hone the back of the iron. A cutting edge is formed by the intersection of two honed surfaces. To hone the back of the iron, place it flat on a medium whetstone. Hone the iron in this position until all of the visible scratches left from the iron's manufacture are removed in the area, starting at the cutting edge and going up the iron about two inches.

Now, switch to the fine stone and hone the same area. Once you have done this, it is not necessary to do it each time you sharpen the iron. The purpose of this step is to remove the grinding marks left on the back of the iron from the surface grinder used at the factory.

Next, sharpen the bevel. Examine the cutting edge; it should be straight and free from large nicks. Check it with a square to make sure that it is straight and square. If you need to square it up or remove large nicks, use the grinder.

The bevel should be ground to an angle between 25 and 35 degrees. The plane will cut soft woods better when the iron is ground to a low angle. When you are working with highly figured hardwoods, an iron with a high angle will better avoid chipping. A good average angle for most work is 30 degrees. If the cutting edge is straight and square, doesn't have large nicks, and the angle is correct, there is no need to grind it; proceed directly to the medium whetstone.

There are two bevels on the cutting edge of the plane iron. The primary bevel is the one made by grinding the bevel. The secondary bevel is made during the honing process. The secondary bevel is a very narrow band that forms the actual cutting edge.

Illus. 2-3. A finely tuned smoothing plane is one of the best tools to use on the wood in preparation for a classic finish.

Hone the primary bevel on the medium stone. Place the iron bevel-down on the stone and rock it back and forth until you can feel that the primary bevel is resting flat on the stone. Now, hold the angle of the iron constant as you move the iron in a straight line back and forth across the full length of the stone. This step will prevent the secondary bevel from getting too wide. After a few strokes, look at the secondary bevel; it should be a narrow band just barely visible behind the cutting edge.

Next, switch to the fine stone and hone the secondary bevel. Place the iron bevel-down on the stone. Rock the iron until you feel the primary bevel resting flat on the stone. Now, rock the iron up about five degrees. Hold this angle constant as you move the iron back and forth on the stone. When a small burr or wire edge forms on the back of the cutting edge, you have honed the secondary bevel enough. The wire edge is a small hook of steel that is bent over when the secondary bevel intersects the back of the iron. You may not even be able to see it, but you can feel it by pulling your fingernail across the edge. If your fingernail catches at the edge of the iron, then the secondary bevel is honed sufficiently.

Now, back-off the iron. This procedure will remove the wire edge. Place the back of the iron flat on the face of the fine whetstone and rub it back and forth a few strokes. Next, use your fingernail to feel for the wire edge. If it is gone from the back of the iron, feel for it on the front of the bevel. Usually the wire edge will bend over to the front. Turn the iron over and hone the secondary bevel again as described above but make only two or three strokes. This should be enough to remove the wire edge completely. If the wire edge has not been removed, repeat the backing-off procedure.

The final step in achieving a very sharp edge is to strop the edge on a leather strop. To strop a plane iron, use a piece of leather about the same size as the whetstones and glue it to a flat piece of hardwood. The leather should be impregnated with a very fine abrasive powder. Jeweller's rouge, silicon-carbide paste, or polishing compound can be used. Apply the abrasive to the leather and rub it in. Place the iron on the strop and use the same procedure described for backing-off the iron. Make sure that all of the strokes are made pulling the iron rearwards. If you push the iron forward, it will cut into the leather. You now have a sharp iron that will leave a smooth surface suitable for a classic finish.

After assembling the plane, adjust it for a very fine cut and manipulate the lateral adjustment until the cutting edge is square to the mouth.

Planing Procedure

To plane effectively, you must clamp the work securely to a sturdy workbench. A bench with an end vise and bench dogs is very useful for planing. Stand close to the bench with your shoulder directly above the work. Stand with your feet about three feet apart, left foot forward. Using this stance, you can put your whole body into the stroke instead of doing all of the work with your arm.

Take a very fine cut in long strokes. The shavings should be as thin as onion skin. Skewing the plane may help it to cut more smoothly. To skew the plane, hold it at about a 10-degree angle to the board but keep the stroke parallel to the board's edges.

It is important to plane with the grain. If you plane across the grain, the chances of tear-out are increased. Tear-out occurs when the wood fibres split along the grain ahead of the plane iron. This will leave a chipped section that will stand out after the wood is polished. At the first sign of a change in grain direction, reverse the plane and plane into the new grain direction. On highly figured wood, it may be impossible to avoid tear-out; in that case, skip this step and use a cabinet scraper instead.

SCRAPERS

A scraper can produce a smooth surface even on highly figured woods. There are two basic types of scraper. The hand scraper is simply a steel blade that is held in your hands. A cabinet scraper has a stock that holds the scraper blade and a small sole to keep the cutting action uniform.

Scrapers work best on hardwoods. They can also be used on softwoods, but their cutting action is not as consistent. A lot depends on the "character" of the board; on some boards, you can get as smooth a surface as produced on hardwood, and on others the scraper will dig in and chatter.

In the past, scrapers were widely used as the final step in surface preparation. With the widespread availability of sandpaper, their use has declined; but they are still the tool to use when you want to make the surface very smooth in preparation for a French-polish finish.

Scrapers have a sharp burr on the edge of the blade that shaves off thin shavings of wood. Sharpening the scraper correctly is the key to achieving good results with it. It is important to remember that the scraper has a cutting edge formed just like any other cutting edge—by the intersection of two honed surfaces. Taking care to sharpen this cutting edge is one of the important steps in sharpening a scraper.

For rough work, the scraper can be sharpened with a file; but to get a very smooth cut, I prefer to sharpen it on a fine whetstone. Begin by removing the old burr. This is done by laying the scraper flat on the face of the stone and rubbing it back and forth.

Next, hone the edge of the scraper. Hand scrapers are honed at a 90-degree angle, cabinet scrapers at a 45-degree angle. To hone a hand scraper, hold the blade straight up on the stone and rub it back and forth. The procedure for honing a cabinet scraper is similar to that used to hone a plane iron. Place the bevel on the stone and rock the blade until you can feel the bevel resting flat on the stone. Now, hone the bevel until a wire edge is formed on the back. Back-off the wire edge as described for plane irons.

The next step in sharpening a scraper is what makes it different from a plane. It is called *burnishing*. The burnishing process rolls the cutting edge over to form a sharp burr on the edge of the blade. This burr is almost microscopic, but you can feel it by drawing your fingernail across the cutting edge.

You will need a rod of hardened steel to burnish the edge. This can simply be the shank of an awl or the back of a gouge, or you can use a special burnisher that looks like a small oval file with no teeth. There are also burnishers that are mounted in a wooden stock that guides them.

You can burnish the edge with the scraper held flat on the workbench and the edge overhanging the bench, or you can clamp it between blocks of wood in a vise.

Wipe a drop of light oil on the burnisher before you begin. First, place the burnisher flat on the face of the blade and pull it along the edge about four times. Next, place the burnisher on the edge of the blade. For a hand scraper, the burnisher will be at 90 degrees. The burnisher will be at 45 degrees if you are sharpening a cabinet scraper. Pull the burnisher across the edge about four times with it held at this angle; then start to roll the burr by lifting the handle of the burnisher slightly on each stroke. After several light strokes, check the burr with your fingernail. When your fingernail catches on the edge, it is time to stop. For a more complete discussion of scraper sharpening, refer to my book *Plane Basics*.

To use a hand scraper, hold it with both hands. Place both thumbs against the middle of the blade. Bow the blade slightly by pressing in the middle with your thumbs. The cut is made with the scraper held almost vertical (Illus. 2-4). The top of the scraper should angle only slightly away from you. You can adjust this angle as you cut to get the best cutting action. Push the scraper away from you in a straight stroke parallel to the grain. If the scraper is cutting properly, fine shavings should curl off.

Illus. 2-4. A hand scraper can be used to remove any marks left by the planes. Hold it in both hands and bow it slightly by pressing in the middle with your thumbs.

Hand scrapers come in various shapes besides the common rectangular one. These curved scrapers are useful for smoothing curved surfaces such as a cabriole leg (Illus. 2-5). They are used in much the same manner as the rectangular scraper, except that it is usually impossible to bow them.

Illus. 2-5. A gooseneck scraper can be used on curved surfaces.

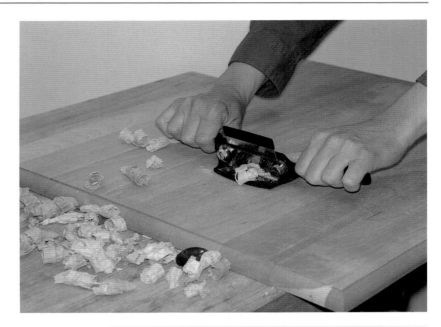

Illus. 2-6. A cabinet scraper has a stock that holds the blade. This makes it better for scraping large, flat surfaces such as tabletops.

Cabinet scrapers have a stock to hold the blade and a setscrew to bow the blade. This makes them less tiring to use. The sole of the cabinet scraper keeps the cutting action uniform. I prefer a cabinet scraper for smoothing a large surface. I use the hand scraper to get into corners and in difficult areas where the angle of the blade must be adjusted to get a smooth cutting action.

To adjust the scraper, first loosen all three screws and place the scraper sole-down on the flat surface of a board. Let the scraper blade rest on the board and tighten the two outside screws. The thumbscrew in the middle adjusts the bow of the blade. The amount of bow determines the depth of cut. Start with only a slight bow and increase it slightly until the cutting action is as desired.

Grasp the handles of the cabinet scraper with both hands and push the scraper in long strokes parallel to the grain (Illus. 2-6).

ABRASIVES

It is often possible to get a smooth, even surface using only planes and scrapers; but if there are rough areas or marks left after the planing and scraping operations, they can be removed with abrasives.

Before sandpaper was developed, other abrasives were used. One of the more interesting abrasives is sharkskin (Illus. 2-7). It was used in a manner similar to sandpaper; however, the cutting action of sharkskin is different from sandpaper. The tiny scales on the dried sharkskin work like the teeth of a rasp. They will only cut in one direction. The sharkskin should be oriented so that the cutting will

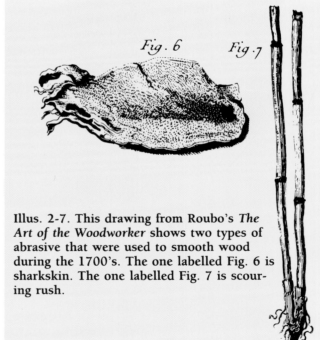

Illus. 2-7. This drawing from Roubo's *The Art of the Woodworker* shows two types of abrasive that were used to smooth wood during the 1700's. The one labelled Fig. 6 is sharkskin. The one labelled Fig. 7 is scouring rush.

take place on the forward stroke in line with the grain. Sealskin was also used as an abrasive.

Sand leathers were another type of abrasive material. These were more often used to smooth between coats of finish instead of the bare wood. A sand leather is a soft piece of leather impregnated with an abrasive powder. Sand, pumice, rottenstone, or tripoli can be used to make

Illus. 2-8. You can gather scouring rush in many places near water. Let the rush dry before use. Break the stems into small pieces and hold them together in a small bundle. Rub the bundle of scouring rush with the grain of the wood. The abrasive grit in the rush will smooth the wood like sandpaper.

a sand leather. The sand leather is usually used wet with water or oil, and new abrasive is added as necessary. Cloth was often used instead of leather with the finer abrasives. Several old books recommend using a tripoli cloth for smoothing between finishing coats.

Another natural abrasive is scouring rush; it is also called Dutch rush or horsetails. This type of plant (genus *Equisetum*) incorporates microscopic pieces of silica in the walls of the hollow tubular stem. Dried scouring rush can be bundled together and used like sandpaper (Illus. 2-8).

The mineral abrasive pumice was also used in the past to smooth the surface of a board. When used to smooth the surface of a board, pumice is used as a stone instead of being ground to a powder. A surface of the stone is flattened by rubbing it against a harder type of stone; then the flat surface of the pumice stone is rubbed over the wood.

By the time *The Cabinet-Maker's Guide* was published in 1825, glass paper was a widely used abrasive. This was the predecessor of modern sandpaper. It was made by gluing ground glass to heavy paper.

Steel wool came into widespread use around 1900. It soon became very popular with wood finishers because it

Illus. 2-9. Steel wool is a traditional favorite of wood finishers, because it conforms to the surface and it won't clog like sandpaper. It is useful for smoothing bare wood and between coats of finish.

will conform to the surface and it doesn't clog (Illus. 2-19). Steel wool is particularly well suited for smoothing between finish coats.

Steel wool is graded based on the size of the steel strands. The coarsest grade used in wood finishing is #2. This coarse grade is only used to remove old finishes with stripper. It will leave deep scratches in bare wood.

A finer grade that can be used to remove the residue left on the wood after most of the finish has been removed with stripper is #0. For smoothing bare wood, use #00. To smooth between coats use #00 or #000. The finest grade is #0000. Use this grade to rub the final coat of a finish to a satin shine.

Steel wool has one drawback: It sheds fine particles of steel as you use it. These particles must be removed from the surface before you apply the next coat of finish. You can remove most of the steel particles with a soft brush. A tack cloth will remove most of the remainder. With oil-based finishes, any remaining particles of steel won't be a big problem; but if you are using a water-based finish, the steel will rust and leave a visible dark spot on the wood. For this reason, I recommend that you don't use steel wool when you will be using water-based products.

Modern technology has come up with a solution to this problem. Synthetic finishing pads are a synthetic substitute for steel wool. They can be used just like steel wool, but they won't leave steel particles behind, so you can use them with water-based products.

In *The Cabinet-Maker's Guide,* a complaint is made that the glass paper of the day was being adulterated with sand. This is probably a description of sandpaper in its early development, possibly as flint paper. The most common type of abrasive used today is sandpaper.

Using Sandpaper

The planing and scraping operations will leave a very smooth surface, so there is no need to start with a coarse abrasive. Usually, you can start with 150-grit abrasive. The plane or scraper will have flattened the surface of the board, so when sanding you should use a padded sanding block so that the sandpaper will conform closely to the surface of the wood. If you have not flattened the surface with a plane or scraper, then you must use a coarse abrasive on a hard block to flatten the surface before proceeding to the fine abrasive and padded block.

If you have done the previous steps well, you won't need to do much sanding; just make a few light strokes with the grain to clean up any remaining marks on the surface. After sanding with 150-grit sandpaper, switch to 220-grit sandpaper for a final smoothing (Illus. 2-10).

Illus. 2-10. If you have planed and scraped the wood first, you won't need to do a lot of sanding. Use a padded sanding block so that the sandpaper will conform to the wood surface.

The next step in sanding is called *breaking the arrises.* An arris is the sharp corner of the wood. If you leave it unbroken, the finish will be very thin at the corners and will soon rub through to bare wood. In some cases, a chamfered or a rounded-over corner is used as part of the design, but usually a sharp corner is wanted.

You can preserve the look of a sharp corner when breaking the arrises by sanding them very slightly with 220-grit sandpaper. Use a sanding block and hold the block at 45 degrees (Illus. 2-11). Just make one continuous pass over the corner. This will be enough to form a small imperceptible flat surface on the corner that the finish can adhere to, but it won't noticeably chamfer or round over the corner.

Many of the natural stains described in this book are water-based. When you apply water to wood it raises the grain. This means that tiny fibres stand up on the wood surface. Even after the wood dries, these raised fibres will remain. This will give the wood a rough surface.

You can help to eliminate grain raising when you apply the stain by dampening the wood with water. Use a sponge to apply the water to the wood (Illus. 2-12). This will raise the grain. Let the wood dry and then sand it smooth with 220-grit sandpaper. You have now removed most of the fibres that will stand up when the wood gets wet, so when you apply the stain there will be much less raised grain.

Even when you raise the grain and sand it smooth before staining with a water stain, there will still be some

Illus. 2-11. Sand the sharp edges on the wood with fine sandpaper on a sanding block held at a 45-degree angle. This is called "breaking the arrises." It rounds the arrises, but preserves the look of a sharp corner.

Illus. 2-12. If you are going to use a water stain, first raise the grain using a sponge dampened with water. Let the wood dry and then sand it lightly with fine sandpaper.

raised grain after the stain dries. Luckily, the classic water stains penetrate deep into the wood, so you can lightly sand the wood after the stain is dry to remove the roughness. Be careful though, because if you sand too hard you will cut through the stain.

For most finishes, the project should be fully assembled before you apply one. However, when you are preparing a project for a French-polish finish, you may choose to leave it partially disassembled. It is possible to French-

polish an assembled piece of furniture, but it is often easier to polish the individual parts before completely assembling the project. After the parts have been smoothed, make a trial assembly (Illus. 2-13). If everything fits correctly, then disassemble the project. Apply masking tape to the joint surfaces. This will prevent polish from getting on them so that the glue will adhere when you make the final assembly.

Illus. 2-13. In most cases you should complete the assembly of the project before you apply the finish. However, if you are going to apply a French-polish finish, you may want to leave the project partially disassembled to expedite the polishing process.

CHAPTER THREE

French-Polishing Supplies

FRENCH POLISHING IS a method of applying many thin coats of shellac using a cloth pad called a "rubber." The prepared shellac is called "polish." The rubber is lubricated with a small amount of oil to keep it from sticking to the previously applied polish. The supplies needed to apply a French-polish finish include the materials used to make the polish, the rubber, and the oil. They are discussed below.

SHELLAC

French polish is made from shellac and alcohol. Shellac is a very desirable finishing material. It forms a tough yet flexible film on the wood. It has high mechanical strength and abrasion resistance. It has very good adhesion properties, and individual coats of shellac bond together. It dries quickly, and it is easy to clean up.

Shellac has proven itself as a finishing material over a long time period. We don't yet know how some of the modern finishes will look in one hundred years, but examples of shellac finishes a hundred years old or older still survive in good condition.

Shellac would probably be considered the ideal finishing product if it weren't for its one deficiency: It is not very water-resistant. If water is allowed to stand on the surface for longer than a few minutes, it will be absorbed into the shellac and cause a milky white spot. When water is allowed to stand on the finish for a long time, it will soak through the shellac film and damage the underlying wood. One of the virtues of shellac is that it is easy to repair and renew the surface when it is damaged. Chapter 6 gives details on correcting defects.

Shellac is produced from a natural resin called lac. Lac is produced by an insect commonly called the lac bug. Lac resin has been used for centuries in the areas where it is produced (India, Thailand, China, and Burma). It has probably been in use for more than 25 centuries in these areas.

The name lac comes from the Sanskrit word *laksa. Laksa* means one-hundred thousand. You can see that the name is appropriate when you realize that it takes about 150,000 lac bugs to produce one kilogram (2.2046 pounds) of shellac.

Swarms of lac bugs attach themselves to trees when it is time for the bugs to reproduce. The lac bugs suck sap from the tree. The sap is chemically transformed in the body of the bug.

Each female lac bug will lay about one thousand eggs. She exudes lac to cover herself and the eggs. The lac from thousands of lac bugs fuses together to form a hard shell over the swarm. The adult lac bugs will die inside the shell of lac; in six or seven months the young lac bugs break out of the lac shell.

After the young have left the lac shell, the twigs covered with lac are harvested. These lac-covered twigs are called "stick-lac." When the lac is broken off the twigs, it is called "grain-lac." At a mill, the grain-lac is ground and sifted and then soaked in water. After the material has been dried, it is called "seed-lac."

Grades of Shellac

- *Seed-lac* is the least-refined grade of lac available. It is the raw material that all other grades of shellac are made from. In the past, seed-lac was held in higher regard than shellac. Stalker and Parker give high praise to seed-lac varnish and advise that shellac is only suitable for use on the inside of drawers, frames of tables, frames of chairs, stools, etc. How can it be that the raw material was better than the refined grades? The answer is that not all seed-lac is alike. The color and wax content of seed-lac varies depending on the area and type of tree it is gathered from and even the individual bugs that made it. Look at the three samples of seed-lac in Illus. 3-1. The sample on the left of the photograph is Siam seed-lac; it has a very dark color. The sample in the middle is Bysaki seed-lac; it is lighter in color. The sample on the right is very light; it is called Kusmi seed-lac.

Stalker and Parker recommend only using the best seed-lac that is large-grained, bright, and clear. As you can see from Illus. 3-1, they were describing Kusmi seed-lac. Most likely, during the 1600's and 1700's, the lightest high-quality seed-lac was used to make varnish or French polish, while the darker varieties of seed-lac were used to make shellac.

There is also considerable variation in color between individual pieces of seed-lac. Each batch of seed-lac will

Illus. 3-1. Seed-lac is the least-refined grade of lac. In this photo, you can compare three types of seed-lac. The Siam seed-lac on the left is a dark brown. The Bysaki seed-lac in the middle is a dark amber. The lightest grade of seed-lac is the Kusmi on the right. Seashells were often used by old-time wood finishers as disposable containers. I'm following that tradition in this book by displaying materials in shells.

contain a quantity of very light-colored pieces; these could have been sorted out by hand to improve the quality of the seed-lac even more. Selecting only the lightest varieties of seed-lac would have made the seed-lac lighter in color than the refined shellac of the period.

Today, seed-lac is not commonly sold to the public, but a few specialty mail-order companies do sell it for those wishing to experiment with it. French polish made from seed-lac produces a slightly different look than polish made from refined grades, and it appears to be slightly more water-resistant (Illus. 3-2). If you are striving for absolute authenticity for an antique reproduction, then you may want to experiment with seed-lac.

• *Button Lac* is produced by the hand method of refining lac. This is the method that was used in the 1600's and 1700's. The seed-lac is placed in a long muslin sack. The sack is about two inches in diameter and may be 25 feet long or longer. One worker holds a section near the end of the sack by an open-hearth charcoal stove. As the heat from the stove melts the seedlac, another worker twists the far end of the sack to squeeze out the melted lac and force more seed-lac into the heated section of the sack. The lac is then formed into discs, called buttons, that are about three inches in diameter. After the lac cools, the buttons are broken into smaller pieces (Illus. 3-3). This method is not used much anymore, so supplies of button lac are limited but still available from specialty wood-finishing supply houses.

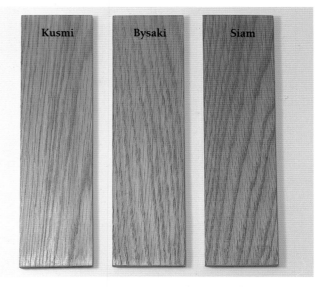

Illus. 3-2. These oak samples have been French-polished with seed-lac polish. The sample on the left is finished with Kusmi polish. The middle sample displays Bysaki polish. The sample on the right is finished with Siam polish. You can see that the Kusmi polish is very light, while the other two darken the wood.

Button lac has a dark brown color. It is usually only used to duplicate an antique finish of similar appearance, because its dark brown color will obscure the color and grain pattern of light woods.

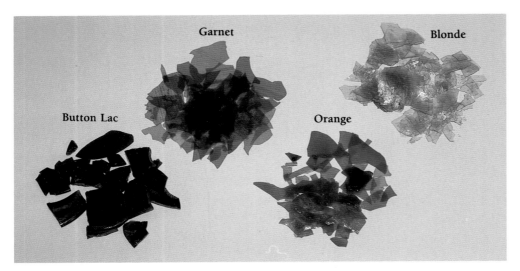

Illus. 3-3. You can still see the rounded edges of the buttons on some of these pieces of button lac on the far left. Dry shellac forms into thin flakes. Garnet shellac flakes are shown second from the left, and orange shellac flakes to the right of them. Blonde shellac flakes are shown on the far right.

• *Orange Shellac* can also be produced by the hand method of refining lac. After the melted lac is squeezed out of the muslin sack, it is stretched into large thin sheets by hand. When the lac hardens, the sheets are broken up into smaller pieces. The thin sheets of lac are called "*shells.*" (The name shellac is a combination of the words shell and lac. In old books, shellac is spelled shell-lac. In French, shellac is called *laque en écailles*. Literally translated, this means "lac in fine sheets.")

Most of the orange shellac available today is made by machine. Either a thermal or a solvent process is used. The thermal process is similar to the hand process. The lac is melted and forced through filtres. While it is still hot, it is rolled into thin sheets. The solvent process uses ethyl alcohol to dissolve the lac. The liquid is then filtered and thickened by evaporation. The thickened shellac is then rolled into thin sheets. When the sheets are hard, they are broken into small flakes.

Orange shellac is a more refined grade of lac than button lac. It still retains some of the orange-brown color of raw lac, but it is a lighter shade than button lac. Orange shellac has been produced by the hand method for centuries, so it is an authentic finish for antiques. Since it lets more of the natural wood color and grain pattern show, it is usually favored over button lac. Orange shellac accounts for the coloration seen in some antique finishes. When it is applied directly to a dark wood the finish will have a warm brown appearance. When it is applied to a light wood such as pine, the result is a medium-amber color (Illus. 3-4).

• *Garnet Lac* is similar to orange shellac in most characteristics, but it is has a deeper brown color. It is a good choice when you want to achieve a true brown color on

dark wood or when you have stained the wood dark and you don't want the shellac to alter the color.

• *Blonde Shellac* is a very light amber color. It can be used on lighter-colored woods without darkening the color. It also produces a very good finish on dark woods, where it emphasizes the natural color of the wood or stain without altering it. Different manufacturers use various names for several grades of blonde shellac. They vary slightly in color, but they are all similar. You can try several different types to find the one you like best. They may be called lemon, super-fine, blonde, or super-blonde.

• *White Shellac* is the lightest type of shellac. It is almost completely clear. It makes a good French polish for marquetry or other applications when you don't want to alter the natural color of the wood. White shellac is produced through a different process than that used for the other grades of shellac. It is dissolved in chemicals that bleach out the color and is then vacuum-dried. The bleaching process chemically changes the shellac. White shellac is only sold in liquid form, because the bleaching makes it insoluble in alcohol unless it is dissolved immediately after the process.

Bleached shellac has been available in the United States since 1849, when William Zinsser established the first United States shellac bleachery in New York. (See *The Story of Shellac* in Bibliography on page 126.) So white shellac is an authentic finish for furniture dated after 1849.

White shellac imparts no color to the wood. It is as clear as modern lacquer. Recently, the Zinsser company has changed the designation of white shellac to clear shellac to differentiate the product from white-pigmented shellac, which is used as a sealer primer under paint.

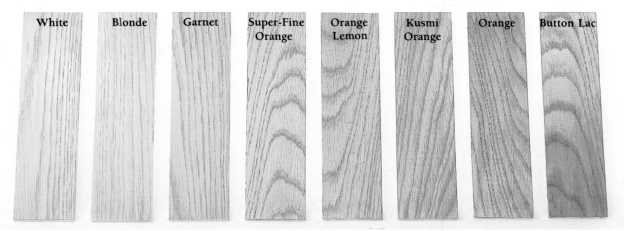

Illus. 3-4. There are many different grades of shellac available. Different manufacturers have slightly different grades and use various names for similar grades, so this topic can be confusing. These oak samples reveal the difference in some of the grades. From left to right, the samples have been French-polished with the following grades of shellac: white, blonde, garnet, superfine orange, orange-lemon, Kusmi orange, orange, and button lac.

White shellac cannot be stored indefinitely. The container will be stamped with an expiration date. In the past, the shelf life was as short as six months, but improvements in the product have extended the shelf life to three years.

Always check the expiration date when you buy the shellac and use it before that date. If you use the shellac past its expiration date, it may never completely dry. You can check to see if it is still usable by applying a coat to a piece of scrap wood. If it dries in two hours or less, it is still usable. If it remains tacky after two hours, don't use it.

• *Modified Shellac* Natural shellac, even the bleached white shellac, contains a natural wax called "lac wax." This is the milky white material that settles to the bottom of shellac that has been on the shelf for a while (Illus. 3-5). When the shellac is applied by the French-polishing process, the wax has no effect on the clarity of the film. However, when the shellac is applied in thick coats as a glaze or spirit varnish, the wax may cause some cloudiness in the film. When the clearest possible finish is required, use dewaxed shellac. In old books, dewaxed shellac is sometimes called "French varnish." Dewaxed shellac is commercially available with a wax content of less than 0.1 percent.

You can make your own dewaxed shellac by letting the wax settle to the bottom of the bottle and then pouring the clear liquid through filter paper. A convenient source of filter paper is the paper filter used in coffee makers.

Natural lac resin contains two types of resin: hard lac resin (HLR) and soft lac resin (SLR). Shellac can be modified by altering the proportions of these two resins. Modified shellac has not been widely used in wood finishing.

Illus. 3-5. Lac contains a natural wax called lac wax. The wax can cause the finish to look cloudy if the film is very thick. Here, you can see how the wax makes the liquid cloudy. Normally, the wax will settle to the bottom of the jar after a while; I stirred it up before taking this photo. The button lac on the far left is so cloudy you can't see any of the plane in the background through the liquid. The blonde shellac in the middle is lighter, but the wax still makes it cloudy enough that you can't make out any details of the plane. The dewaxed shellac on the right is so transparent that the plane knob is clearly visible through the liquid. Dewaxed shellac is more transparent, so it is better for glazes that are applied in a thick coat.

It is usually used in other industrial processes. The use of modified shellac in wood finishing is an area that could use more research and experimentation.

Commercially Prepared French Polish

Commercially prepared French polish is available. Some of these products are simply standard shellac that has been dissolved in alcohol and cut to the correct consistency for French polishing. Others are blends of shellac with other resins and other ingredients that add desirable properties to the polish. Since the products differ from one manufacturer to another, choosing one is a matter of individual preference and experimentation.

The products available in Great Britain are usually labelled French polish. In the United States, they may only be identified by a trade name. Commercially prepared polish is often useful when you will only be doing a small amount of French polishing and you don't want to bother with mixing your own. If you choose to use a commercially prepared French polish, be sure to follow the directions on the container; some types contain ingredients that make the use of oil as a lubricant unnecessary.

PREPARING FRENCH POLISH

The Cabinet-Maker's Guide includes a formula for French polish made from several different resins. (See accompanying box, Illus. 3-6.) However, French polish is usually made using shellac alone.

During the time when French polishing was at its zenith, many types of shellac were available as ready-to-use liquids as well as in the dry form. Now that shellac is not as popular as it once was, only orange shellac and white shellac are available in liquid form; the other grades of shellac are usually sold in dry form that must be dissolved in alcohol before use. Seed-lac comes as small grains that look like seeds. Button lac comes as small chunks that resemble broken glass. The rest of the grades are available in flakes. I find that garnet and blonde shellac are the two most useful grades (Illus. 3-7).

SOLVENTS

Shellac is soluble in a variety of solvents, but the traditionally accepted solvent to use for French polish is ethyl alcohol. In old books, this is called "spirits of wine," because it is the type of alcohol found in wine. The alcohol used as a solvent for shellac must be very pure and free from water. Water in the alcohol will turn the shellac cloudy. An old-time test for the alcohol was to place a pinch of gunpowder in a spoon and cover it with alcohol, and then light it on fire. If the gunpowder would ignite

THE
Cabinet-Maker's Guide:

The True French Polish.

To one pint of spirits of wine, add a quarter of an ounce of gum copal, a quarter of an ounce of gum arabic, and one ounce of shell-lac.

Let your gums be well bruised, and sifted through a piece of muslin. Put the spirits and the gums together in a vessel that can be close corked, place them near a warm stove, and, frequently shaking them, in two or three days they will be dissolved; strain it through a piece of muslin and keep it tight corked for use.

Illus. 3-6. This excerpt from *The Cabinet-Maker's Guide* contains instructions for making a French polish from several different resins.

Illus. 3-7. Even though there are many grades of lac products, I find that you can do most work using these two: garnet shellac and blonde shellac. Garnet shellac is good for dark wood, and blonde shellac works well on lighter wood. Most French polishers prefer to buy shellac in flake form. The flakes are dissolved in alcohol before use. In this photo, you can see the difference in color between the garnet flakes and the blonde flakes.

after the alcohol had burned off, then the alcohol was good enough to use. If the gunpowder didn't ignite, then there was water in the alcohol.

Nowadays, you can buy alcohol specifically made as shellac solvent that has the correct properties, so you don't need to perform this test. Alcohol sold as a solvent must be rendered undrinkable by law. This is done by the addition of small quantities of other poisonous liquids. Ethyl alcohol that has been mixed with these poisonous substances is called denatured alcohol or proprietary solvent. It is best to use a shellac solvent recommended by the shellac manufacturer, because some of the denaturing compounds can have an adverse effect on shellac.

The best solvent for shellac is pure ethyl alcohol, but

by law this cannot be used. Companies that make liquid shellac are allowed to use a grade of alcohol that has a smaller quantity of the denaturing compounds than can be legally sold to the public. Even though there is a certain mystique about dissolving your own shellac in flake form, when a liquid shellac is available, it will actually be slightly superior because of the quality of the alcohol used as a solvent.

The amount of dry shellac flakes and solvent determine the "cut" of the liquid shellac. Cut is a way to classify the consistency of the liquid polish. A four-pound cut is a thick liquid and a one-pound cut is almost as thin as water. The designation comes from the fact that mixing one pound of shellac flakes with one gallon of alcohol will make a one-pound cut, four pounds of shellac flakes in a gallon of alcohol will make a four-pound cut, etc. It is not necessary to use a full gallon, as long as you keep the proportions the same.

Most French polishing is done with a one-pound or a two-pound cut. The usual custom is to initially make a quantity of four-pound-cut shellac and then thin it to the desired cut in smaller amounts as needed.

To make one quart of four-pound-cut shellac, weigh 12 ounces of shellac flakes and put them in a glass container. Measure three cups of alcohol and pour them over the flakes. Let the flakes dissolve overnight. You can occasionally shake the container, if the flakes clump together, to speed up the process. After the flakes are thoroughly dissolved, strain the liquid through several layers of cloth. Store the mixture in a tightly closed glass container.

Metal containers should not be used to store shellac. The shellac will react with the metal and corrode it. This can discolor the shellac. Commercially prepared shellac may be available in a metal can, but the interior of the can has been coated with a special coating to prevent corrosion.

When you are ready to polish a project, dilute some of the four-pound-cut shellac by adding additional alcohol. Experienced wood finishers often don't need to measure the ingredients; instead they can judge the consistency by the way it pours from a bottle or by rubbing it between their thumb and finger. However, at first it is best to accurately measure the shellac and alcohol so that you can achieve consistent results.

You can use any convenient-size measuring cup. To dilute four-pound-cut shellac to a three-pound cut, add one-fourth measure of alcohol to a full measure of four-pound-cut shellac. To dilute four-pound-cut shellac to two-pound cut, add three-fourths measure of alcohol to one full measure of four-pound cut. To dilute four-pound-cut shellac

Illus. 3-8. Old wine bottles have traditionally been a favorite container for liquid shellac. Glass bottles with cork stoppers are ideal for shellac storage because there is no metal to come into contact with the shellac. Ordinary metal containers can cause discoloration of the shellac. The metal cans used for commercially prepared shellac have a special coating inside to prevent this.

to one-pound cut, add a full measure of alcohol to one-half measure of four-pound-cut shellac.

If you are starting with three-pound-cut shellac, you can dilute it to two-pound cut by adding three-eighths measure of alcohol to a full measure of three-pound-cut shellac. To dilute three-pound-cut shellac to a one-pound cut, add three-fourths measure of alcohol to one-half measure of three-pound-cut shellac.

Store the diluted shellac in a glass container. The traditional container preferred by French polishers is an old wine bottle (Illus. 3-8). For storage, keep the bottle tightly corked. You can make a convenient dispenser by cutting a small groove along the side of a cork. This will allow you to pour out a few drops of polish as needed while keeping the alcohol from evaporating (Illus. 3-9).

OIL

Oil is used as a lubricant in the French-polishing process.

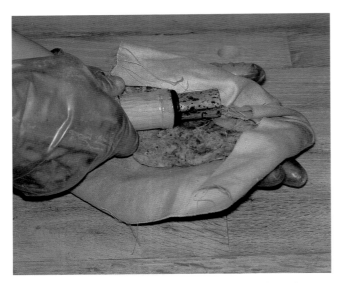

Illus. 3-9. A groove cut in the side of a cork makes a convenient dispenser for filling the French-polishing rubber with shellac. Open the rubber, place the groove against the back of the wadding, and let the shellac soak into it. For long-term storage, use an ungrooved cork.

Only a tiny amount of oil is used and it is removed from the surface at the end of the polishing process. Some people believe that the oil mixes with the shellac, but this is not correct; the oil is simply a lubricant to aid in the application of the shellac.

In France, the preferred oil is a mineral oil called paraffin oil. In Great Britain and the United States, the traditional oil is linseed oil. The preferred type of linseed oil is raw linseed oil. This is linseed oil that has not been processed to make it dry more rapidly. Boiled linseed oil has been processed to make it dry more quickly.

Boiled linseed oil is used for an oil finish, but it is not usually used for French polishing. Some people, however, do use boiled linseed oil in French polishing with good results. Since the oil does not actually become a part of the finish, the type of oil used is not critical as long as it lubricates the rubber sufficiently. Some finishers even use lemon oil as the lubricant. Lemon oil is really just paraffin oil with a lemon extract added.

PAD

French polish is applied with a cloth pad. In France the pad is called a *tampon*. The British name for the pad is a "rubber." In the United States both names are widely used, or it is simply called a French-polishing pad. Throughout this book I will use the name rubber for the French-polishing pad, except when I am specifically discussing the French method; then I will refer to the pad as a tampon.

The rubber (Illus. 3-10) consists of two parts: the inner wadding and the outer cover. The wadding is made from wool or cotton. Wool tends to feed the polish out faster than cotton. The choice depends on your personal preference. I suggest that you experiment with both until you form your own opinion.

Wool used for the wadding can be the raw wool directly from the shearer, wool yarn, or pieces cut from an old wool sweater. If you use wool yarn, cut it up into short lengths and wad it together. Use raw cotton such as the cotton found as padding in some upholstered furniture for the wadding. Although each polisher has his or her own personal preference, generally wool is used with the French method and cotton with the British method of French polishing.

Before using cotton or wool to make a rubber, it should be broken in. Soak the wadding material with one-pound-cut shellac, then wring out the excess and let the wadding air-dry until it feels dry to the touch on the surface but wet as soon as you apply some pressure to it. Break in

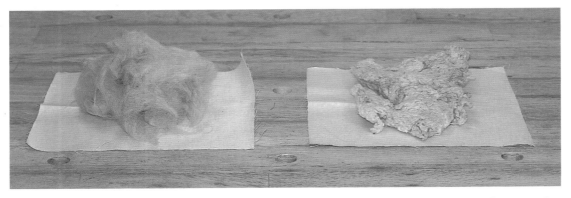

Illus. 3-10. A rubber consists of an outer linen cover and an inner wadding made from wool (left) or raw cotton (right).

enough material to make several rubbers and keep it in an airtight container. The wadding should never be allowed to dry out completely. If it does, throw it away.

The cover of the rubber can be made from any tightly woven lint-free material, but linen is the traditional favorite and it will last longer than any other type of cover.

To make a rubber, use a ball of wadding about 2½ inches in diameter. Raw cotton won't compress very much, so you can start with a piece the size of the finished rubber. Raw wool will compress a lot. Start with a ball about 4 inches in diameter and compress it to 2½ inches.

Place the wadding in the center of a piece of linen about 9 inches square. The size of the rubber can be varied to suit your personal preference and the size of the object that you will be polishing, but the sizes given above seem to be a good average size for most work. Some polishers prefer a ball-shaped rubber, but the most widely used types are the pear-shaped and the egg-shaped rubbers (Illus. 3-11).

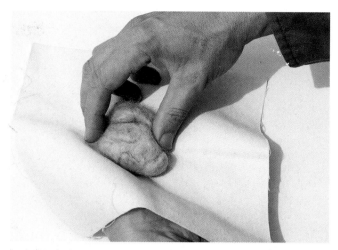

Illus. 3-12–3-15. Making an egg-shaped rubber. To begin making it, place a 2½-inch-diameter ball of broken-in wadding in the middle of a 9-inch square of linen.

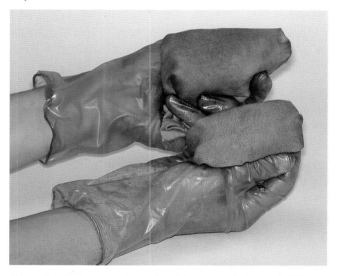

Illus. 3-11. A pear-shaped rubber (top) is useful for getting into corners and details. An egg-shaped rubber (bottom) is easier to make and is useful for polishing large surfaces.

The pear-shaped rubber has a narrow end that is useful for getting into corners. The egg-shaped rubber is useful for large, flat surfaces such as tabletops. Illus. 3-12–3-21 are step-by-step photos that show how to make both types of rubber. After making a rubber, keep it in a tightly capped glass jar so it won't dry out (Illus. 3-22). You can reuse a rubber many times if it is kept from drying out.

When you add shellac to the rubber, open the cover and add the shellac directly to the top of the wadding.

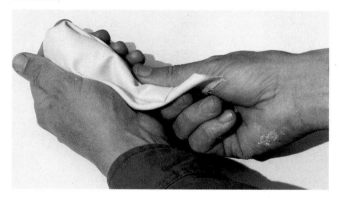

Illus. 3-13. Wrap the cover around the wadding, leaving a "tail" of cloth at the rear.

Illus. 3-14. Twist the tail to tighten the cover on the rubber.

Illus. 3-15. Fold the tail over the top of the rubber. This illustration shows how to grip the rubber. About two-thirds of the rubber is in the palm of your hand; the bottom third of the rubber extends past your fingertips. As you work, you can squeeze the sides of the rubber with your fingers and thumb to control the amount of shellac that is fed out through the bottom.

Illus. 3-16–3-21. Making a pear-shaped rubber. Start with a 2½-inch ball of broken-in wadding and squeeze it into a pear shape. Place the wadding in the middle of a 9-inch square of linen.

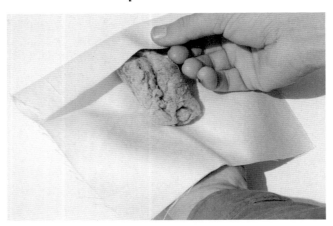

Illus. 3-17. Fold over 1 inch of the cover at the small end of the wadding.

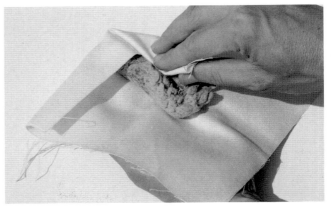

Illus. 3-18. Now, fold over one of the front corners at a 45-degree angle.

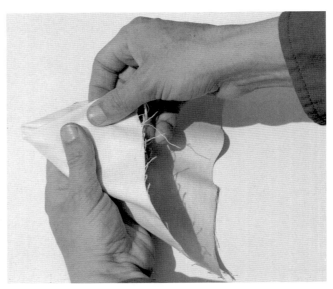

Illus. 3-19. Fold over the other front corner at a 45-degree angle, to, make a point.

Illus. 3-20. Twist the tail to tighten the cover on the rubber.

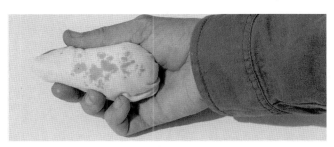

Illus. 3-21. Fold the tail over the top of the rubber and grip the rubber like this. Your forefinger should rest on top of the pointed end of the rubber.

Illus. 3-22. When properly cared for, rubbers will last a long time. In fact, they seem to get better with age. Store the rubbers and extra broken-in wadding in a sealed glass container.

Never pour shellac onto the face of the cover. One of the keys to the French-polishing process is ensuring that the rubber slowly dispenses a small amount of shellac in a controlled manner. If the face of the rubber is wet with shellac, the shellac is being fed at much too rapid a rate.

POUNCE BAG

In the first stage of French polishing, a fine-powdered filler is used. In the French method, fine pumice powder is used. The British method calls for plaster powder. Red-clay brick ground to a fine powder can also be used for a red mahogany finish.

You can simply sprinkle the filler on the surface, but a pounce bag (Illus. 3-23) makes it easier to apply the filler. In the French method, the pounce bag is called a *couille*. The pounce bag is simply a piece of cloth about 10 inches square. The cloth will act as a filter. Loosely woven cloth will let the pumice flow out freely. Closely woven cloth will only let out the finest particles. Pour a pile of the powder in the middle of the square and then lift the corners of the cloth and make a ball. Tie the bag closed with a piece of string.

To apply the filler to horizontal surfaces, shake the pounce bag over the work. To apply the filler to vertical surfaces, gently pat the pounce bag against the wood. The powder will filter through the cloth and be deposited on the work.

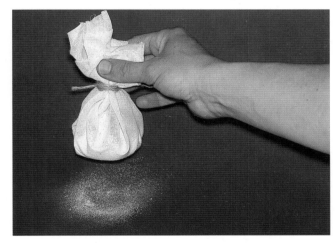

Illus. 3-23. A pounce bag is a convenient way to store and dispense pumice or other fine powders. The cloth acts as a filter that won't let any coarse particles get on the surface of the work.

CHAPTER FOUR

The French-Polishing Process

FRENCH POLISHING PROBABLY came into widespread use in the mid-1800's. *The Cabinet-Maker's Guide,* published in 1825, refers to it as "of comparatively modern date." (See Illus. 4-1.)

There are four steps in the French-polishing process: filling, bodying, stiffing, and spiriting off. Filling, the first step, consists of filling the pores of the wood so that they won't show through the finish. In the next step, bodying, the majority of the polish is applied to build up the film thickness. Stiffing is the process of smoothing and polishing the surface of the film. The final step is spiriting off; in this step, the remaining oil from the previous steps is removed from the surface.

THE

Cabinet-Maker's Guide: Friction varnishing, or French polishing.

GENERAL OBSERVATIONS.

THE method of varnishing furniture, by means of *rubbing* it on the surface of the wood, is of comparatively modern date, though bees'-wax has been used either by itself, or mixed with spirits of turpentine for a very considerable period, for that purpose, and which at first produces a very good gloss, though it does not wear well, and is particularly liable to spot with wet, and look smeary when touched with the fingers; to remedy these inconveniencies, and put a harder face, which shall not be so liable to scratch as varnish, and yet have an equally fine face, the French polish was introduced, and as it would be unpardonable in a work like this, to omit a full direction of the process, and also the various preparations of the different compositions necessary, it is here introduced that nothing might be wanting to make this work as complete as possible.

All the polishes are used pretty much in the same way, therefore a general description will be a sufficient guide for the workman. If your work is porous, or the grain coarse, it will be necessary, previous to polishing, to give it a coat of clear size previous to your commencing with the polish, and when dry, gently go over it with very fine glass-paper, the size will fill up the pores and prevent the waste of the polish, by being absorbed into the wood; and also a saving of considerable time in the operation. Place your work so that the light may shine on it in an oblique direction to enable you

to see by looking sideways, how the polishing proceeds.

Make a wad with a piece of coarse flannel or drugget, by rolling it round and round, over which, on the side meant to polish with, put a very fine linen rag several times doubled, to be as soft as possible, put the wad or cushion to the mouth of the bottle containing the preparation, (or polish,) and shake it, which will damp your rag sufficiently, then proceed to rub your work in a circular direction, observing not to do more than about a square foot at a time; rub it lightly till the whole surface is covered, repeat this three or four times, according to the texture of the wood; each coat to be rubbed until the rag appears dry, and be careful not to put too much on the rag at a time, and you will have a very beautiful and lasting polish; be also very particular in letting your rags be very clean and soft, as the polish depends in a great measure on the care you take in keeping it clean and free from dust during the operation.

Illus. 4-1. This excerpt from *The Cabinet-Maker's Guide* confirms that French polishing came into widespread use in the 1800's.

There are two different methods of applying a French-polish finish: the French method and the British method. Each of the methods has its own merits. If you are concerned with historical accuracy, then your choice will depend on the method that would most likely have been used originally. When historical accuracy is not an issue, I suggest that you experiment with both of the methods and choose the one you like better. The French method is very good when no stain is used under the polish. It enhances the natural color of the wood and brings out the subtle beauty of the grain. The British method works well on wood that has been stained.

French polishing should be done in a well-lighted, dust-free room. Lighting is important because you must be able to see any minor irregularities in the film surface immediately in order to take corrective action. The best place to work is near a window. The light from a window comes in at an angle so that you can sight across the surface of the work and get a good reflection. This will reveal any surface defects.

The worst type of lighting is overhead fluorescent lighting. Overhead fluorescent lighting is so flat and uniform that it will hide small surface defects. If you use such lights, position them away from the work area so that the light hits the work at about a 45-degree angle.

The room temperature and humidity are also important. The best working temperature is around 70 degrees Fahrenheit (22 degrees Celsius). Don't work in a room that is colder than 40 degrees Fahrenheit (5 degrees Celsius) or hotter than 95 degrees Fahrenheit (35 degrees Celsius).

Humidity will affect the drying time. When the humidity is low, you can work faster because each coat of polish will dry quickly. When the humidity is high, you must wait longer before you go back over the surface. You should allow the surface to "rest" whenever you are having problems because the film is not drying quickly enough. You should usually let the work rest overnight between the steps of filling, bodying, stiffing, and spiriting off. If everything goes well, you can do a rush job all in one day, but I don't recommend it as a usual practice.

The reason a French-polish finish is so glassy smooth is that the finish is applied under pressure from the rubber. In order to apply the correct amount of pressure, you must clamp the work firmly to a solid work surface. This is very different from most other finishing procedures, where only the lightest touch is used to apply the finish. If it is possible, you should do much of the polishing before the project is assembled. This will allow you to polish the surfaces flat on the bench instead of vertically, and you won't have as many inside corners to deal with. Apply masking tape to joint surfaces before you begin to polish the work. This will leave bare wood for the glue to adhere to when the project is assembled.

You will need a good workbench and ways to secure the work to the bench. At first, practise on flat pieces of scrap wood. These can be held in place with an end vise and a bench dog. Large, flat parts can be secured by fastening temporary cleats to the underside of the work. Even though the underside doesn't need the high degree of finish that the top will receive, it should be sealed with several coats of polish. These can be simply applied with the fad as described later. After it has thoroughly dried, attach two cleats to the underside of the work. Keep the cleats slightly shorter than the width of the work so that they won't interfere as you polish the edges.

Now, place the work on the bench and clamp the cleats between the end vise and bench dog. With the work secured this way, the edges are raised up off the bench so you can easily polish them. Once you have some experience on large, flat surfaces that can be easily secured, you can work on the more awkward parts. They are discussed in the next chapter.

USING THE RUBBER

Using the rubber correctly is one of the most important aspects of French polishing. The rubber is more than just a rag used to wipe on a coat of liquid; it is a sophisticated applicator that feeds out polish at a controlled rate. Old-time polishers always held the rubber in their bare hands, but the shellac makes a sticky mess on your hands and the alcohol can dry out your skin. I recommend that you wear thin plastic gloves. They will protect your hands and yet they are thin enough to still let you feel the action of the rubber.

Always open the cover and add shellac directly to the back of the wadding (Illus. 4-2). After reclosing the cover, grip the rubber with your whole hand, wrapping your fingers and thumb around the sides (Illus. 4-3). Press the face of the rubber against the palm of your other gloved hand or a scrap of board to distribute the new shellac throughout the wadding.

As you grip the rubber, the pressure you apply to the sides of the rubber controls how much polish feeds out through the face of the rubber. When the rubber has just been filled with shellac, very little pressure is needed. As the shellac is fed out of the rubber, gradually increase the pressure you exert with your fingers and thumb to keep the feed rate constant.

The rubber should never be so wet that polish oozes out of the sides. If it does, it will run down onto the work

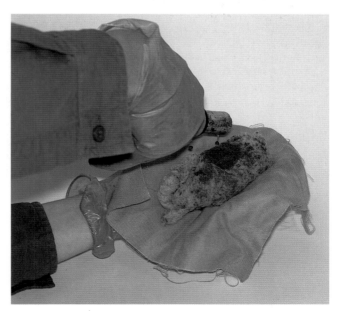

Illus. 4-2. Add shellac to the rubber by opening the cover and pouring the shellac onto the back of the wadding.

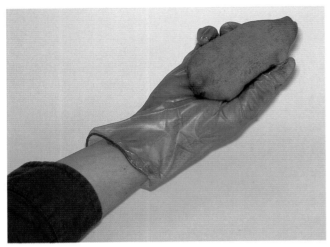

Illus. 4-3. Grip the rubber like this.

and leave little ridges on the surface called "whips." If you do get whips on the surface, release the pressure on the side of the rubber and immediately wipe over the whips. If you wipe them up quickly enough, no damage will be done. That is why proper lighting is so important. You must be able to see the smallest defect as soon as it occurs if you are going to be able to correct it easily.

An important rule to remember is never to let the rubber stand still on the work. If you let it stand in one place even for a moment, you will dissolve the underlying layers of polish and ruin the job. Start a stroke with the rubber in midair and lower it to the work while it is in motion. To remove the rubber from the work, lift it while still continuing the stroke in order to finish the stroke in midair.

It is also important to learn how the rubber should feel when you are using it correctly. The rubber does not glide freely across the work; there is a definite resistance when you are exerting the right amount of pressure and using just the right amount of oil. One way to recognize this feeling is to wipe the palm of your dry hand across a piece of clean, dry glass. That is about the same amount of resistance you will feel when you are using the rubber correctly.

There are several different motions used to move the rubber across the surface of the board. A circular motion is used for filling and bodying. Make sure that you go over the edges and corners as frequently as the rest of the surface. This can be done by making a series of small circles around the edges after each series of larger circles over the rest of the work. Occasionally alternate to a long figure-eight pattern. The purpose of changing the motion occasionally is to prevent any ridges from forming in a particular pattern.

When there are ridges left on the surface, it is called "ropiness." Any ropiness formed by one pattern will be flattened out by the following pattern. This process is called "pulling over."

Long oval strokes with the grain are used in the final stages of bodying. If ropiness occurs during this stage, you can return to the circular motion occasionally for pulling over the ropiness. Straight strokes with the grain are used for stiffing and spiriting off.

THE FRENCH METHOD

As the name implies, French polishing originated in France. Actually in France it is not called French polishing; it is called *vernis au tampon*. *Vernis* means varnish or polish. In French, a wood finisher is called a *vernisseur*. The pad used to apply the polish is called a *tampon*. In the French method, each coat of polish is very thin. The result is a very delicate-looking finish.

Filling

Open-grained woods such as mahogany and walnut have large pores that must be filled in order to achieve a glass-smooth surface film. Even closed-grained woods such as birch and maple have microscopic pores, and there are small scratches left from sanding.

The first stage in French polishing is to fill all of these small depressions in the surface up to the level of the surrounding wood. Some type of fine powder is usually used to fill the pores. In the French method, the powder used is pumice. In earlier times, brick dust was also used as a filler on mahogany (Illus. 4-4). Brick dust is made by breaking a red-clay brick into small pieces and then grinding it to powder with a mortar and pestle. The powder is placed in a *couille* (pounce bag). The couille filters the powder so only the finest brick dust is sprinkled on the surface of the work.

Pumice is a very good filler, because when it is mixed with shellac it changes from a white powder into a translucent material that lets the natural color of the wood show through. Also, since pumice is an abrasive, the filling process smooths the surface of the wood and removes the tiny scratches left by the last grade of sandpaper. As the pumice abrades the wood, the wood fibres mix with the pumice, giving the filler the same appearance as the surrounding wood. The result is the most natural-looking grain filler available.

In the French method, straight alcohol is occasionally added to the tampon to dilute the shellac. One way to keep from getting the bottles of shellac and alcohol confused is to use a clear wine bottle for alcohol and a green one for shellac (Illus. 4-5). Cut a V-shaped groove in the side of the cork on both bottles to make dispensing the liquid easy. For dark-colored woods, use garnet or orange shellac. The color of the shellac will help to color the filler, making it match the surrounding wood better. For light-colored wood, use blonde or white shellac. Dilute the shellac with alcohol to get a two-pound cut.

Make a tampon to use for the filling operation as described in Chapter Three. For the French method, use wool for the wadding. Make sure that the wadding has been broken in. Filling is hard on the tampon cover, so use a strong piece of cloth.

Open the cover of the tampon and wet the wadding with alcohol (Illus. 4-6); then pour on an equal amount of two-pound-cut shellac. Squeeze the tampon to mix the alcohol and shellac. Adding alcohol and shellac to the tampon separately allows you to vary the consistency of the polish as necessary throughout the process.

Illus. 4-4. Brick dust can be used as a filler for red mahogany.

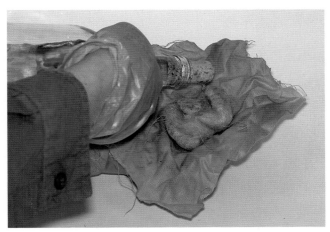

Illus. 4-6. Pour the alcohol onto the wadding first, and then add the shellac.

Now, grip the rubber and use a circular motion to wipe a thin coat of shellac on the surface of the wood (Illus. 4-7). The polish will dry quickly at this stage, so you can go over the surface again as soon as you have finished wiping on the first coat. Apply three thin coats.

The French method uses paraffin oil as a lubricant. After you have applied three thin coats of polish without any oil, it is time to add some oil to the tampon. The fingertip method is a convenient way to determine the correct amount of oil. For the filling stage, use three fingertips of oil. With a plastic glove on your hand, dip three fingertips into the oil, and then wipe all of the oil from your fingertips

Illus. 4-5. In the French method, alcohol is added to the tampon to dilute the shellac. It is traditional to use a clear wine bottle to dispense the alcohol and a green wine bottle to dispense the shellac.

Illus. 4-7. The first step in filling is to apply three thin coats of shellac to the bare wood with the tampon.

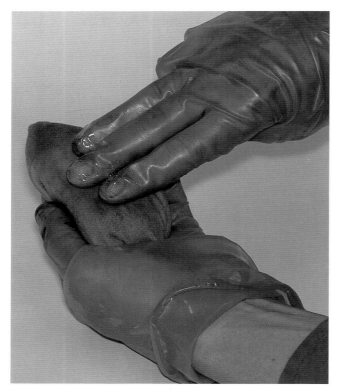

Illus. 4-8. The fingertip method is a good way to measure the amount of oil needed for each step. Use three fingertips of oil for the filling step.

on the face of the tampon (Illus. 4-8). The oil is important to the filling process. It helps to keep the surface smooth as the filler builds up in the pores.

Now, sprinkle a little bit of pumice on the surface of the wood (Illus. 4-9). It is better to use too little pumice than too much. You can add more if necessary, but if you use too much you can end up with little lumps of pumice left on the surface. If you can't wipe the lumps off, they must be sanded off with fine sandpaper.

Illus. 4-9. Sprinkle a little pumice from a *couille* (pounce bag) on the surface.

Using a circular motion, rub the tampon all over the surface of the wood (Illus. 4-10). As you rub, the pumice will abrade the wood surface, smoothing out small scratches left by the last grade of sandpaper and creating a filler made from wood dust, pumice, and shellac. Press down hard on the tampon to force this filler into the pores of the wood. As the tampon dries out, add more alcohol and shellac. At this stage, you are not trying to build a film of polish, so don't add very much shellac. If the pumice is accumulating on the surface of the work, add another fingertip of oil to the tampon.

Keep rubbing the surface until you can't see any pores or scratches left on the surface when you look at it obliquely and see the light reflected in the surface. If necessary, add more pumice to fill pores that remain open. When the surface looks as smooth and flat as a sheet of glass, you can stop.

Pumice will fill the small pores of closed-grained woods in one application. For wood with larger pores such as

Illus. 4-10. Work the pumice into the pores by rubbing the tampon in a circular motion.

Illus. 4-11. When all of the pores have been filled, let the shellac dry for several days; then smooth the surface by lightly rubbing it with #00 steel wool or a synthetic finishing pad.

mahogany, it may take two or three applications of filler to completely fill the pores.

Put the tampon in an airtight container and let the work rest overnight between each application. The filler will shrink as the shellac dries, so you may think the pores are completely filled, only to discover the next day that the filler has sunk partway into the pores. When you have applied several coats of filler, it is a good idea to allow two or three days for the filler to dry completely before you proceed with the bodying. When the filler is dry, rub the surface lightly with #00 steel wool or a synthetic finishing pad before you begin the bodying (Illus. 4-11).

If you want to use the French method over a stain, the filling step is different. Use a chemical or dye stain that will penetrate deeply into the wood. (See Chapters Ten and Eleven.) Fill the tampon with two-pound-cut shellac and, using long, straight strokes, rub the shellac onto the surface. Don't go over the surface repeatedly; just wipe the shellac on, and then stop and let the surface rest for at least one hour. Now, sprinkle some pumice on the surface and add a little oil to the tampon. Proceed with the filling step as described above, but be careful that you don't rub so hard that you rub through the stain.

Bodying

Bodying is the next step in the French method of French polishing. This is the stage when most of the film thickness, or body, of the finish is built up. Use a tampon that you have reserved for bodying and stiffing. Open the cover

and feed the tampon with about two teaspoons of alcohol and one-half teaspoon of two-pound-cut shellac. Always add the alcohol first and then the shellac. Squeeze the tampon to mix the alcohol and shellac. What you are doing is cutting the shellac further in the tampon. The result at this stage is about a half-pound cut. As the bodying process proceeds, you will slowly decrease the amount of alcohol until you are adding one part alcohol to one part shellac. This will result in about a one-pound cut. Apply two fingertips of paraffin oil to the face of the tampon (Illus. 4-12).

Move the tampon over the surface of the board in a circular pattern at first (Illus. 4-13). As the alcohol evaporates from the shellac, the oil film will be visible on the surface of the work. This visible oil is called a "cloud." If you can clearly see a cloud, then you are doing the work correctly. If clouds don't appear, feed a little more alcohol to the tampon. If you still don't see clouds, try adding another fingertip of oil. You will have to experiment at first to get the right proportions of oil, alcohol, and shellac.

At this stage, the alcohol will evaporate quickly, so you can go back over the surface almost as soon as you finish the first complete coverage. Temperature and humidity will play a role in how fast you can work.

It is important that you let each coat dry before you wipe the tampon over the area again. If the surface has not dried sufficiently, instead of applying a thin layer of

Illus. 4-12. Bodying requires less oil than the filling step did. Use two fingertips of oil for bodying.

Illus. 4-13. Begin bodying by rubbing the tampon in a circular motion.

shellac you will probably wipe off a layer. When conditions are right, you can start at one side of the board and it will be dry by the time you reach the other side, so you can work without interruption.

There will probably be enough oil left on the tampon to last through most of the bodying. Each time you feed the tampon, decrease the amount of alcohol a little until you are adding one part alcohol and one part shellac. As the film of shellac builds, you will feel increasing friction on the tampon. Remember the example of rubbing your

hand across a sheet of glass. If the friction exceeds that amount, then it is time to add oil to the tampon. Dip the tip of your finger in paraffin oil and press your finger in the middle of the tampon face. That amount of oil is all that is needed for quite a while. If the friction becomes excessive again, add another fingertip of oil.

During the first stages of bodying, use a circular motion. Occasionally switch to a figure-eight motion to pull over any ropiness. As the bodying progresses, gradually stretch out the circles into long ovals. Towards the end of the bodying, the stretched ovals will cover the full length of the work and evolve into long, straight strokes, ending in a short curve that transitions to the return stroke.

As you work, keep an eye on the light reflected across the surface of the board. If you see any imperfections in the surface, correct them immediately. Also watch for clouds on the surface. If clouds do not appear, then add more alcohol to the tampon. The formation of the oily clouds is an indication that the process is proceeding correctly.

When you feel that the finish is thick enough, feed the tampon one last time with alcohol only. Work over the surface with long figure-eights until the tampon is fairly dry. Now, let the work rest until tomorrow.

Stiffing

Stiffing doesn't add much to the body of the finish; the purpose of this step is to smooth and polish the film that was laid down yesterday during the bodying. Use the same tampon that you used for bodying. Feed it with one part alcohol and one part shellac at first, and gradually decrease

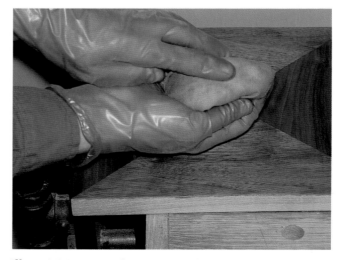

Illus. 4-14. You only need one fingertip of oil on the tampon for stiffing.

the amount of shellac until you are using straight alcohol. Place one fingertip of oil on the face of the tampon (Illus. 4-14). This should be all the oil necessary during the stiffing process.

Start out using long figure-eight motions. At first, it will feel just like a continuation of the bodying. As the tampon dries out, increase the pressure you apply to it. This is where stiffing really begins. Work in long, straight stokes across the surface (Illus. 4-15). The clouds of oil on the surface will become thinner as you work. When it is time to feed the tampon, add just a small amount of alcohol and shellac so that the tampon remains fairly dry.

With each stroke of the tampon, the oil clouds will decrease and the finish will take on a higher gloss. Keep up the stiffing until there is only a trace of oil on the surface.

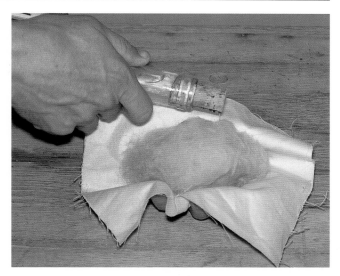

Illus. 4-16. Use a separate tampon for spiriting off. Do not add any shellac or oil to this tampon. Use only alcohol to dampen the tampon.

Illus. 4-15. Stiffing polishes the finish to a high gloss.

Spiriting Off

All that is left to complete the finish is to remove the last trace of oil from the surface. In the spiriting-off step, straight alcohol (spirit) is used to wipe away the last of the oil. Use a separate tampon exclusively for spiriting off. The wool in this tampon should not be broken in with shellac (Illus. 4-16).

Feed the tampon with straight alcohol. Glide the tampon across the work in long, straight strokes without any downward pressure. The tampon should just barely touch the surface (Illus. 4-17). Continue to spirit off the surface until the last trace of oil is gone and the surface glows with a brilliant high gloss.

Illus. 4-17. Spiriting off requires a light touch. Start and end each stroke in the air, and then lightly touch down on the surface with the tampon still in motion.

BRITISH METHOD

The British method of French polishing produces a thicker coat of shellac. The French method can be used with stain, but it is difficult to keep from rubbing through the stain during the filling operation. The British method is well suited for use on stained wood (Illus. 4-18), because a thick coat of shellac is applied over the stain before any significant rubbing is done. Any type of stain can be used

Illus. 4-18. The British method works well with wood that has been stained. Here I am staining the wood with dragon's blood spirit stain, but any type of stain can be used under French polish. See Chapters Ten and Eleven for staining instructions.

under a French-polish finish. (For details on staining, refer to Chapters Ten and Eleven.)

The British method uses plaster filler. This will fill the pores of open-grained woods with large pores, such as oak, better than the pumice filler used in the French method. Raw linseed oil is the preferred lubricant for the British method of French polishing.

Fadding

After the stain is dry, the surface of the wood is covered with two thick coats of shellac. The shellac is applied with a "fad" (Illus. 4-19). The traditional fad is a piece of raw cotton that has been broken in with two-pound-cut shellac. You can also use a piece of soft cloth as a fad. The raw cotton may shed fibres on the finish, so the cloth is easier to use. To make a cloth fad, cut a piece of cloth about 10 inches square and fold it into a pad.

Break in either type of fad by soaking it with two-pound-cut shellac; let the shellac dry for a few hours, and then soften the fad as necessary with alcohol. Grasp the fad in your hand and press it against a piece of wood to flatten its face and mould the fad to the shape of your hand.

Illus. 4-19. In the British method, the first coats of shellac are applied with a "fad." The traditional fad is made from raw cotton (top). You can also make a fad by folding a soft cloth into a pad (bottom).

Fill the fad with two-pound-cut shellac by pouring the shellac on the back of the raw cotton fad (the part you grasp in your hand). Fill the cloth fad by unfolding it and pouring shellac inside the fold (Illus. 4-20).

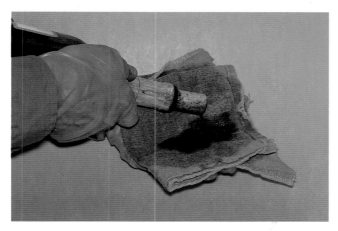

Illus. 4-20. Pour shellac inside the fold of the cloth fad. The fad should be well soaked with shellac so that it will lay down a heavy coat.

Now, wipe the fad across the surface of the wood in long, straight strokes (Illus. 4-21). Start the stroke in mid-air past one edge of the board; come down lightly on the edge of the board with the fad in motion and complete the stroke by going past the far edge. The fad will release the shellac much faster than a rubber.

Each stroke of the fad will lay down a heavy coat of shellac, so very little downward pressure should be used on the fad. At this stage, no oil is used with the fad.

After completing one stroke, begin the next, slightly overlapping the previous stroke. Then stop and let the first coat dry. Depending on the conditions, this may take from 15 minutes to an hour. Then, using the same procedure, apply a second coat.

Now, let the work rest overnight. If you are using a closed-grained wood such as birch or maple, you can skip the filling step; the thick coats of shellac are sufficient filler for closed-grained woods. Just sand the shellac with 220-grit sandpaper to smooth it. For open-grained woods such as oak or mahogany, the next step is filling.

Filling
The traditional filler used with the British method is plaster

Illus. 4-21. Wipe the fad over the wood in long, straight strokes.

of Paris. The plaster must be mixed with a water-soluble stain to make it match the color of the wood. In earlier days, the stains used were not lightfast. After years of exposure to sunlight, the colors faded, leaving the white plaster visible in the pores of the wood. You can see this effect on some antiques.

Modern aniline stains, which are lightfast, can be used. Mix the dry powdered stain with water. Put some dry plaster in a shallow dish. Dip a rag in the water stain and wring it out so that it is just damp. Press the rag into the dry plaster. It will pick up some of the plaster.

Now, wipe the plaster onto the face of the board in a circular motion (Illus. 4-22). As you wipe, the dry plaster will turn into a thick paste as it combines with water stain from the rag. Work over a small section of the project, forcing the plaster into the pores. Before the plaster has a chance to set, wipe off the excess with a rag. Repeat the procedure on the next section of the project until the entire surface has been filled.

Allow the filler to set overnight; then dampen a rag with raw linseed oil and wipe the surface of the board. This will remove the haze of plaster left there and accentuate the color of the stain in the plaster. Let the oil soak into the plaster for a while and then wipe off as much as you can with a dry rag. Examine the surface carefully. It may be necessary to sand the surface flat with 220-grit sandpaper.

After the filler has dried, apply more shellac with the fad. Feed the fad some one-pound-cut shellac and touch the face of the fad with a fingertip of raw linseed oil (Illus. 4-23). Rub the fad over the surface in a circular pattern until it is well coated. Let the surface rest for 15 minutes to an hour and then repeat the procedure.

Let the surface rest again and sight across it. If there are no visible depressions over the pores, you can proceed to bodying. If there are some small depressions, use the fad to apply another coat of shellac. If that doesn't make the surface smooth, let the work rest overnight; then sand the surface with 320-grit wet or dry sandpaper lubricated with raw linseed oil. (In earlier days, a pumice stone would have been used.) Wipe off the oil and proceed with the bodying.

Bodying

Bodying is done with a rubber made with raw-cotton wadding and a linen cover. Open the cover and feed the rubber with one-pound-cut shellac. Touch the face with two fingertips dipped in raw linseed oil. Start applying the polish

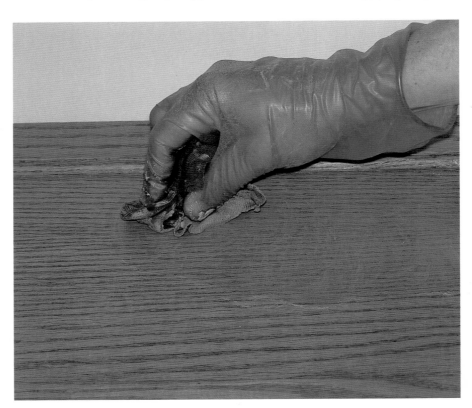

Illus. 4-22. Plaster mixed with water stain is the traditional filler used for the British method of French polishing. Rub the plaster into the pores using a circular motion.

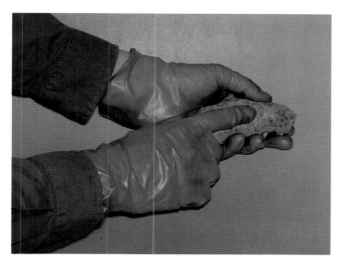

Illus. 4-23. After the filler has dried, apply more shellac with the fad. This time, add one fingertip of oil to the face of the fad.

with a circular motion (Illus. 4-24). Don't add more polish until the rubber is fairly dry; then add a little more polish as needed. Watch for clouds of oil as described in the French method. The rest of the bodying is very similar to the French method. As the bodying progresses, keep elongating the circles until you are making long ovals the length of the work. Occasionally switch to a figure-eight pattern.

If there is some ropiness, revert to the circular pattern to pull over the ridges. If the rubber doesn't pull enough, add a pinch of pumice. The pumice is placed inside the rubber. Remove the cover and sprinkle the pumice on the inside of the face area of the cover. When the rubber is treated this way with pumice, it is called a "grinder" (Illus. 4-25). Make a grinder and keep it in an airtight container, ready to use when necessary. Only use the grinder long enough to remove the ropiness; then switch back to the rubber.

After each feeding, the pressure applied to the rubber should be very light. As the rubber dries out, increase the pressure gradually until you are applying quite a bit of downward force to a fairly dry rubber; then feed the rubber again. If good clouds aren't being produced on the surface and the rubber isn't gliding across the work smoothly, add a fingertip of oil to the face of the rubber. If the surface seems to be soft, let the surface rest for 15 minutes to an hour. Keep up the bodying until you are satisfied with the surface and the thickness of the polish. Now, let the surface rest overnight.

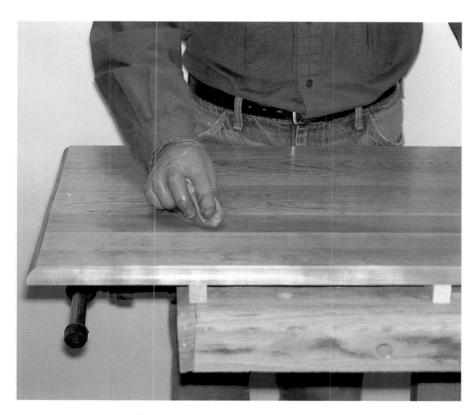

Illus. 4-24. Rub the rubber in a circular motion to start the bodying step.

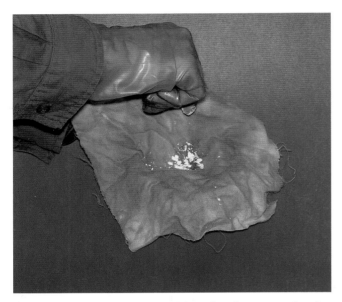

Illus. 4-25. A grinder is a rubber that has a pinch of pumice placed inside the cover. Use the grinder to pull over ropiness.

Stiffing

Stiffing gives the surface its final polish. Use one-pound-cut shellac that has been diluted with an equal measure of alcohol. Use a rubber that you have reserved just for stiffing; this rubber is called a "stiffer." Shape it and flatten its face by pressing it against a board. Don't add any oil to the stiffer. Work the stiffer in long, straight strokes with the grain. Start at one edge and make overlapping strokes until you reach the other edge; then repeat the stiffing process (Illus. 4-26).

The stiffer will gradually pick up most of the oil; as this happens, there will be more resistance on the stiffer (it will get stiff). After you have stiffed the surface completely about four times, most of the oil should be gone and the surface should have a high gloss. Some polishers are able to remove all of the oil during the stiffing process, but usually you will need to proceed to the spiriting-off process.

Spiriting Off

The spiriting-off procedure will remove the last trace of oil from the surface and leave it mirror-smooth. Use a clean rubber that has not been used with shellac for spiriting off. Feed it with a small amount of alcohol.

The spiriting-off rubber used in the British method should be a little drier than the spiriting tampon used in the French method. Wipe the rubber across the work in

long, straight strokes that begin and end in midair off the edges (Illus. 4-27). Apply light pressure to the rubber, using slightly more pressure than you did for the French method at this stage. Work progressively from one edge to the other with overlapping strokes until all traces of the oil cloud are gone.

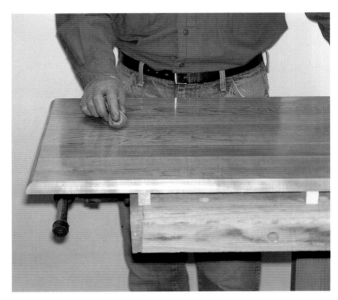

Illus. 4-26. Stiffing polishes the finish. Use long, straight strokes.

Illus. 4-27. Spirit off the last traces of oil using a clean rubber dampened with alcohol.

CHAPTER FIVE

Special French-Polishing Situations

THE PRECEDING CHAPTER dealt with the basics of the French-polishing process and how to apply a French polish to a large, flat surface. This chapter examines ways to apply French polish to awkward places and some variations on the basic French-polishing process.

POLISHING AWKWARD PARTS

Most furniture consists of more than just large, flat surfaces. There are inside corners, narrow edges, carvings, mouldings, and turnings to deal with. Below is a description of how to deal with these different surfaces.

Polishing Into Corners

Polishing into corners takes a special technique because you must keep the rubber in constant motion. If you let it stand still even for a moment, part of the finish will be lifted or a lumpy deposit of polish will develop. The inside corners should be rubbed as often as the rest of the project or else they will be dull compared to the other areas.

Illus. 5-1. Use the pointed end of a pear-shaped rubber to get into corners. Press your forefinger on the tip of the rubber. Always keep the rubber moving.

The pear-shaped rubber should be used when there are inside corners on a project. Place your forefinger at the tip of the pointed end of the rubber (Illus. 5-1). Each time you make a complete pass over the surface of the work, make a pass to the corners. Make sure that the sides of the rubber are clean, because if there is a buildup of shellac on them, it will rub off on the side of the corner. Hold the point of the rubber against the side and guide the point directly into the corner. Now, without hesitating at all in the corner, change directions and slide the point along the other side out of the corner.

For stiffing and spiriting off, you need to use a different technique. Start with the point of the rubber in the corner and then make the stroke out from the corner. If the opposite edge is open, just run the stroke off the edge as usual. If there is an inside corner on the opposite side, when you reach the middle end the stroke by gradually lifting off the surface as you continue the motion of the stroke. Then repeat the procedure starting in the other corner, so that the two strokes overlap in the middle.

Polishing Drawer Fronts and Legs

Parts such as drawers and table legs can present a problem, because they are difficult to hold stationary as you polish them. A few special fixtures will simplify the task. For drawers, attach some overhanging cleats to the bench top (Illus. 5-2). You can slide the drawer opening over the cleats. This puts the drawer face at a convenient working height and holds it securely enough for you to apply the polish.

Table legs have to be finished on all four sides. A cradle will make it more convenient to work on them. Put a nail or screw in the top and bottom of the legs to rest on the cradle (Illus. 5-3). Hold the head of one screw and press the other end firmly against the cradle to keep the leg stationary as you apply the polish, then twist the leg a quarter of a turn and polish the next face. You can make a simple rack to hang the legs up on to dry so that none of the surfaces are marred. The screw fits into a saw kerf on a thin board attached to the wall.

On a small part such as a leg, after a few polishing

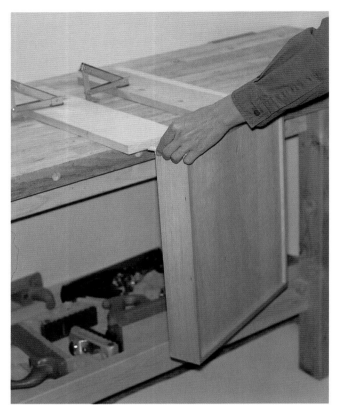

Illus. 5-2. To polish a drawer face, clamp cleats to the bench top and hang the drawer from the cleats.

strokes the surface will have to rest before you can continue the polishing. With a rack and cradle, it is easy to work all four legs at once. By the time you have polished the fourth leg, the first one has rested enough.

Polishing Turnings on the Lathe

French polish is an ideal finish for lathe work. You can polish the project while it is still on the lathe. The French method works better than the British method.

Run the lathe at its slowest speed. Begin by wetting a small tampon with alcohol and shellac. Press the tampon against the rotating turning. Move the tampon back and forth until the wood is evenly coated with shellac (Illus. 5-4).

Next, stop the lathe and use a *couille* (pounce bag) to apply pumice. Apply some paraffin oil to the tampon. Turn the lathe back on and start the filling step.

This process is generally the same as the process described in Chapter Four. The only difference is that the lathe is rotating the work, so you only need to press the tampon against the wood and move it from side to side. It is best to hold the tampon on the underside of the turning so that it is being pulled away from you.

Continue with the rest of the steps as described in Chapter Four. All of the steps except for spiriting off are done with the lathe running. To spirit off the work, use very light pressure on the tampon and turn the lathe slowly by hand.

Illus. 5-3. It is often easier to polish furniture legs before the project is assembled. Make a wood cradle like this to hold the leg while you polish it. Nails or screws in the ends of the leg fit into notches in the cradle.

Illus. 5-4. You can apply French polish to turnings while they are still on the lathe. Use the slowest lathe speed. Apply the polish with a tampon while the lathe is turning.

Polishing Edges

Even the simplest project such as a tabletop will have edges that must be polished. If the edges are flat, you can polish them along with the top, but it is hard to get a good buildup on them. Moulded edges present another problem because the rubber can't get into all of the depressions in the moulding. The process of ''glazing'' is used to apply a finish to parts such as edges, carvings, and mouldings that can't be effectively polished with the rubber (Illus. 5-5).

Usually the glaze is made from a heavier cut of the same type of shellac as used for the polish. A three-pound-cut

shellac makes a good glaze. In the past, copal varnish or gum benzoin was also used as a glaze. Glaze isn't quite as clear and does not have as delicate a luster as French polish, but the difference usually isn't noticeable, because the surfaces it is used on are either small or have a different texture, such as the surface of a carving.

Shellac that is applied by French polishing has a clarity that is hard to achieve with other processes. Part of this results from the way the shellac is fed into the rubber. Natural shellac contains a wax called ''lac wax.'' This wax gives the liquid shellac a cloudy appearance. When the shellac is brushed on, the wax is trapped in the film and makes the shellac film slightly cloudy. This cloudiness is not too noticeable in thin film, but it will become more apparent when thick coats are applied. When you pour the shellac into the back of the rubber, it has to pass through the wadding before it is applied. This wadding acts as a filter, removing some of the lac wax. The result is that a film of shellac applied by French polishing will have greater clarity than a film of equal thickness applied with a brush or fad.

You can get greater clarity in a glaze by using dewaxed shellac. You can buy dewaxed shellac or make your own. To make dewaxed shellac to use as a glaze, strain the shellac through filter paper. You can use the type that chemists use, but an easily available substitute is a paper filter used in automatic coffee makers. Place the filter paper inside a funnel and pour the shellac through the filter.

Glaze is applied with a soft fad. The French use a similar tool called a *mèche*. The *mèche* is a piece of cheesecloth folded into a pad. For very intricate parts, a piece of velvet can be used. The pile of the fabric acts like tiny brush bristles to get into small details on the work. White velvet is best to use, because the dye of colored velvet may be

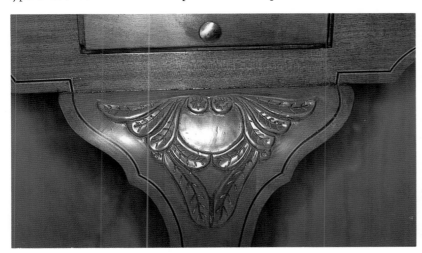

Illus. 5-5. Carvings and intricate mouldings are difficult to polish with a rubber. Areas such as the carving on this leg are usually glazed by applying three-pound-cut shellac with a soft cloth or a brush.

Illus. 5-6. Dark brown or black wax hides imperfections around details. It will also accentuate the details better.

soluble in alcohol and impart a color to the glaze. Glaze can also be applied with a brush.

Wipe on the glaze with a slight amount of pressure. The glaze is spread on more like varnish instead of rubbed in like French polish. Two or three coats of glaze will equal the film thickness of many coats of French polish.

Even when glazing, it may be difficult to get all the way into the tightest details. A trick used by old-time polishers was to use a dark wax after the finish had dried to hide imperfections in the details. For dark woods, use either a dark brown or a black wax (Illus. 5-6). With a soft cloth work the wax into all of the corners and details; then buff the wax off as completely as you can. A small amount of the wax will be left in the inaccessible places. This hides any rough or dull areas left after glazing and also accentuates nicely the details of the work. See Chapter Nine for more details on waxes.

Glaze was often used to finish the interior of drawers. The traditional glaze for this purpose is a three-pound-cut button lac. It is applied in a heavy coat with a fad or *mèche*.

Let the glaze dry until it is almost hard but still slightly tacky. Now, sprinkle powdered talc from a pounce bag over the glaze (Illus. 5-7). Old books call talc powder "French chalk." The talc powder gives the glaze a smooth satin surface. After the glaze is dry, wipe off the loose talc. When you look at an old drawer, you can still sometimes find traces of the talc powder in the rear corners.

FRENCH-POLISHING VARIATIONS
The French-polishing methods described in Chapter Four are probably the most useful and historically accurate methods, but there are several variations on the traditional process that are useful for producing different effects. The variations given here are polishing over oil, open-pore polishing, eggshell gloss polishing, and ebonizing French polish (Illus. 5-8).

Polishing Over Oil
French polish can be applied over a coat of oil. The oil brings out the color and grain pattern of the wood. You

Illus. 5-7. You can give drawer interiors a traditional finish by applying three-pound-cut button lac with a soft cloth fad or a brush. When the button lac is almost dry but still slightly tacky, sprinkle an even coating of talc powder from a pounce bag over the entire surface. After the button lac is completely dry, wipe off the excess talc. The talc gives the button lac a satin finish.

Polish Over Oil   Open Pore   Eggshell   Ebonized

Illus. 5-8. These samples show four variations of French polishing. Left to right: French polish over linseed oil, open-pore French polish, eggshell gloss French polish, and colored French polish.

can use boiled linseed oil or Danish oil under French polish. You can also use a tinted oil to stain the wood if desired.

If you are applying a *clear* linseed or Danish oil, apply one coat of oil and let it dry overnight; then apply another coat of oil and follow the rest of the directions given in Chapter Four. Boiled linseed or Danish oil is used only during the filling step; change to paraffin oil or raw linseed oil for the remaining steps.

If you want to stain the wood with *tinted* oil, the filling step is different. Apply a wet coat of oil to the wood and sprinkle pumice on top of the oil. Make up a tampon that has no shellac or alcohol in it. Rub the tampon over the surface exactly as described in Chapter Four, but add no alcohol or shellac. You are making a filler paste from wood dust and pumice as before, but are using the oil, instead of shellac, as a binder. The dye in the tinted oil will color the filler so it will match the rest of the wood perfectly. After filling the wood, let the oil dry for a day or two before progessing to the bodying. The bodying step and the remaining steps are the same as described in Chapter Four.

Open-Pore Polish

The open-pore polish became popular in the early 1900's. If you are reproducing furniture from that era, this would be a historically accurate finish. It is also useful on any type of furniture.

In the open-pore process, no attempt is made to fill the grain. The open pores of the wood show through to the final surface. The surface has a soft lustre that is slightly glossier than a satin finish but is not a high gloss (Illus. 5-9).

For an open-pore finish, the surface of the wood should be extremely smooth. Instead of stopping the sanding at 220-grit sandpaper, sand the surface an additional time with 320-grit sandpaper. After sanding, remove all of the sanding dust from the pores of the wood. A shop vacuum with a brush attachment can be used for this.

No pumice or oil is used in the open-pore technique. Begin the process with the bodying step, skipping the filling step entirely. The procedure for the bodying step is the same as given for the French method of French polishing in Chapter Four, except no oil is added to the tampon. You must allow the surface to rest longer between each complete coverage of the surface, because the tampon will stick to the surface if the film is not dry enough.

The procedure for the stiffing stage is also the same as that given in Chapter Four, except that no oil is used. Let the surface rest a few minutes any time the tampon starts to drag too much on the surface. Stop the stiffing when you have achieved a soft, low lustre; you are not trying to produce a high gloss. There is no need to spirit off an open-pore polish.

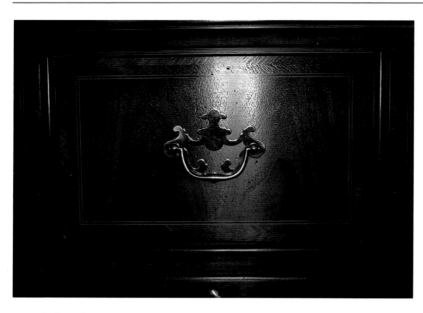

Illus. 5-9. Open-pore French polish. You can see the pores of the wood in the areas where light is reflected.

Eggshell Gloss Polish

The eggshell gloss finish has a smooth surface with no open pores showing, but it has a satin gloss (Illus. 5-10). This is a finish that has only been used since the beginning of the 20th century. It is historically accurate for furniture dating from 1900 to the present.

Follow the directions given in Chapter Four up through the stiffing stage. After stiffing, let the work rest for at least two days. Now, make a tampon from clean material that has no shellac or alcohol on it. Pour some paraffin oil on the tampon. Sprinkle pumice on the surface of the work. Rub the tampon over the work in long, straight strokes. Add oil as necessary to keep the tampon moving freely.

The pumice will remove the gloss and polish the surface to a satin sheen.

Continue the rubbing until the surface has a uniform appearance. Don't rub more than necessary, because you are removing some of the finish with each stroke. It is possible to rub through to bare wood, if you are not careful.

Remove the pumice and as much of the oil as possible with a clean rag. Now, sprinkle some tripoli on the surface. Tripoli is a fine-abrasive powder. It will absorb the remaining oil. Wipe off the tripoli with a soft cloth. Finally, apply a coat of wax and buff it to a satin lustre. (See Chapter Nine.)

Illus. 5-10. Eggshell gloss French polish. This finish is rubbed to a satin gloss with pumice.

Coloring French Polish

French polish can be colored with the addition of pigments or dyes. Pigments mixed with shellac have been used for as long as shellac has been in use. Pigmented shellac is actually a type of paint, but it can be applied using the French-polishing technique; therefore, the surface finish is suitable for fine furniture.

Any color pigment can be used, but the most popular is black. Until modern lacquers took over the job, black-pigmented shellac was used as a piano finish.

- *Ebonizing* is a term that is used for several different wood-finishing procedures that produce a black finish. When used in conjunction with French polishing, it describes a procedure that uses black-pigmented shellac to produce a rich, black finish.

Ebonized finishes were very popular during the Victorian period. Dry, powdered pigments should be used with shellac. For ebonizing, use carbon black pigment. This pigment is also called lampblack, because a common way to produce it was to place a sheet of steel in the flame of a gas lamp. After a while, a thick deposit of black soot would accumulate on the steel. When it had cooled, the lampblack was scraped from the steel and mixed with the shellac. Today, you can buy ready-made carbon black pigment. Add the pigment to a small quantity of one-pound-cut blonde shellac.

Choose a closed-grain wood for ebonizing, unless you want the grain pattern to show through for a special effect. Begin by staining the wood with black stain. (See Chapters Ten and Eleven.) When the stain is thoroughly dry, start polishing, skipping the filling stage and proceeding directly with the bodying.

To produce a very deep ebony finish, you will have to use many coats of black shellac. Apply as much as the surface will take in a day; then let it rest overnight and repeat the procedure daily until you are satisfied with the finish. Then proceed to the stiffing and spiriting-off steps.

You can produce a high-gloss black finish like the type characteristic of a piano finish, or you can give the surface an eggshell finish that is more characteristic of real ebony. Follow the directions given for the eggshell finish above, but be very careful not to rub too hard, especially at the arrises. It is easy to rub through at the arrises and show the white wood below.

- *Alcohol-Soluble Aniline Dye* is used to give a transparent color to shellac. This alcohol-soluble dye is available in many wood tones and bright colors. It is also called "spirit stain." The stain can be used to give the finish the appearance of an old, darkened finish, to blend light and dark areas of a board to the same tone, or to produce interesting decorative effects using bright colors. There are also some natural stains that are alcohol-soluble. (See Chapter Ten for details.)

The dye comes as a powder. First, dissolve the dye in straight alcohol; then add the alcohol to the shellac until the desired color intensity is achieved. You can also keep the liquid stain in a separate bottle and add it to the tampon instead of alcohol. This technique is useful when you are trying to blend light and dark areas of the wood to the same shade. You can add more stain to the tampon when you are working on the lighter areas and less when you are working over dark wood.

If you want all of the wood to receive the same amount of stain, use the stained shellac for the filling and bodying steps. For blending, use shellac without the stain for the filling step and add the stain to the tampon as needed during the bodying step. In either case, use straight shellac for the stiffing.

CHAPTER SIX

Correcting French-Polishing Defects

BESIDES BEING A beautiful and durable finish, French polish has another advantage: It is easy to touch up defects in the finish. Whether the defects appear soon after applying the finish or are the result of time and wear, you can repair a French polish finish easily, and usually the repair will be completely undetectable. The reason French polish is this forgiving is because the shellac can always be softened with a fresh application of alcohol, and new coats of shellac applied over old ones will fuse together no matter how old the undercoating of shellac is. This makes it possible to completely repolish a piece of furniture without stripping the old finish.

Sweating, clouding, dullness, scratches, and cracks are five common French-polishing defects. Methods for correcting these defects are given below.

SWEATING

Sweating is a defect caused by improper technique during polishing. If too much oil is used, or you didn't completely remove all of the oil during the polishing process, oil may appear on the surface at a later date. Remove the oil with a rag moistened with vinegar. Spirit off the surface again if necessary.

CLOUDING

When shellac absorbs moisture, it turns translucent-white. This is called clouding. If clouding occurs soon after applying the finish, it may have been caused by applying the finish over a water stain that had not dried sufficiently. Clouding can also occur when the polishing is done in an extremely humid environment.

If clouding occurs long after the finish has been applied, it is probably caused by water left standing on the finish. When water is spilled on a French-polish finish, no harm will be done if it is wiped up immediately; but if it stands on the finish for a while, the shellac will absorb some of the moisture and cloud up. You should always use a coaster under a glass placed on a French-polished surface to avoid glass rings, which are ring-shaped clouds.

Pure alcohol will absorb moisture, so it is sometimes possible to remove cloudiness by spiriting off the surface using the same technique described in Chapter Four on page 41 (Illus. 6–1). If that doesn't help, then try polishing the area with a very fine abrasive such as rottenstone mixed with paraffin oil. This will remove a layer of the finish. If the clouds are near the surface, you will be able to polish them off without serious damage to the finish. If the clouds are deep, then this method won't work. In severe cases, it may be necessary to repolish the surface as described later.

Illus. 6-1. A rubber moistened with alcohol will sometimes remove cloudiness from the finish. Use the same technique described on page 41 to spirit off the surface.

DULLNESS

When a freshly polished surface turns dull after a few days, it is usually because you have used too much oil and have not removed it completely. You may mistake oil on the surface for a high-gloss finish, not thinking to remove it. After a while, the oil will dull.

To remedy this dullness, wipe the surface with a rag dampened with vinegar. This will remove the oil film. Now, look at the surface and note how the polish was really applied. If it is acceptable, just give it a coat of paste wax and buff it out. Now that the oil is gone, you may find out that you didn't really do as good a job as you thought you did. In that case, repeat the stiffing process, being sure to use only a touch of oil, and then spirit off the surface.

Dullness on an old finish is the result of many minute scratches on the surface caused by years of wear. You may be able to restore the gloss by rubbing it with rottenstone and paraffin oil or a commercially prepared polishing compound. Remove all of the oil with a rag dampened with vinegar and then apply paste wax. If the scratches are too deep, you can apply a new coat of polish following the procedure given later in this chapter.

SCRATCHES

Large scratches that cut through to the underlying wood can't be rubbed out. The process used to repair scratches is not difficult, but it is often hard to get the scratch to match the surrounding finish. Before you try this technique on an important project, experiment on something unimportant.

Deep scratches that extend below the wood surface must be filled. Apply stick shellac of the appropriate color with a hot burn-in knife. For details on this process, refer to my book *Wood Finisher's Handbook*. In this book, I will describe a repair for scratches that damage the French polish but not the underlying wood. Use a small artist's brush to apply four-pound-cut shellac to the scratch (Illus. 6-2). Try to keep the fresh shellac inside the depression of the scratch and not on the surrounding finish. Let the shellac bulge up above the surrounding surface a little.

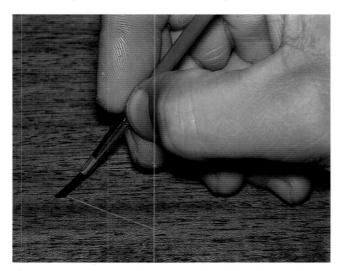

Illus. 6-2. Small scratches can be repaired with an artist's brush. Use the brush to fill the scratch with thick shellac.

Let the shellac dry overnight. If the repair has sunk below the surrounding surface, apply another coat and let it dry overnight. Now, dampen a rubber with a little alcohol and rub it over the repair to cut it down to the same level as the surrounding finish and blend it in (Illus. 6-3). Be careful not to rub through the surrounding finish. Let the repair rest overnight. If it is dull, polish it with polishing compound and apply paste wax.

Illus. 6-3. After the shellac in the scratch is dry, rub over the scratch with a rubber moistened with alcohol. This will level the shellac in the scratch with the surrounding finish. Be careful not to rub too hard on the surrounding finish or you may rub through to the wood.

CRACKS

Shellac is slightly elastic, so it can move with the wood as it shrinks and swell during changes in humidity, but eventually over many years, the wood movement may cause tiny hairline cracks to appear in the surface. Unless the cracking is severe, it is usually left alone because it adds to the patina of age. Removing the patina on a valuable antique can lower its value, so I don't recommend repolishing a valuable antique simply because the finish has hairline cracks (Illus. 6–4). When cracking occurs on a newer piece or if other finish damage makes a complete repolishing necessary, follow the directions below under the Repolishing head.

Applying a fresh coat of French polish over hairline cracks will often make the cracks disappear or at least make them less noticeable (Illus. 6-5). If repolishing doesn't help, or if the cracks reappear after a while, then you need to reamalgamate the finish if you want to com-

Illus. 6-4. Minor cracks and scratches in the finish of this antique chest add to its patina of age. Don't repolish an antique simply because it has minor defects like hairline cracks.

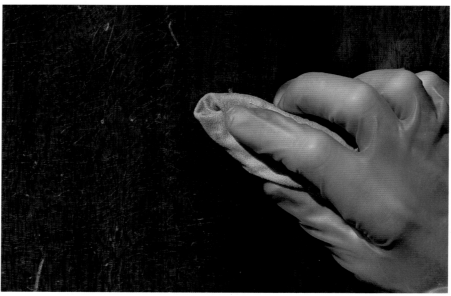

Illus. 6-5. Sometimes all it takes to repair a damaged finish is another coat of French polish. This finish has hairline cracks. A fresh coat of polish softened the old finish enough to fuse most of the cracks and make the remaining ones much less visible.

pletely remove the hairline cracks. Directions for reamalgamating the finish are given later in this chapter.

REPOLISHING

No matter how old a shellac finish is, it can be softened with alcohol (Illus. 6-6); this means that you can add a new coat of polish at a later date without a lot of sanding or other surface preparation. The old finish should be clean and free from wax or oil buildup. Wiping the surface with a rag dampened with vinegar is usually a sufficient means of cleaning.

When repolishing, it is usually best to use blonde or white shellac. This will preserve the original color of the finish. Begin the polishing process as if you were halfway through the bodying stage. The only difference is that you should not use any oil at this stage. Oil used at first would seep through the cracks and darken the underlying wood.

Just apply the new polish right on top of the old one. The new shellac and alcohol will soften the underlying finish and cause hairline cracks and minor surface defects to fuse together. You don't need to apply many coats, since the original finish provides most of the body. Once you

Illus. 6-6. Repolishing can bring a dull, damaged finish back to life.

have built up a new film on the surface, you can add a touch of oil if you need it. When you are happy with the results, start the stiffing. Finish by spiriting off just as described in Chapter Four.

REAMALGAMATING

If there are deep clouds or other defects, they may not be completely removed by simply applying additional layers of polish on top of the old finish. Try the method described above under the Repolishing head first; if you can't get the defects cleared up during the bodying stage, then you may want to try reamalgamating. This is the most drastic method described here, but it is less damaging than stripping and refinishing the project.

Reamalgamating the finish will preserve the original color and many of the marks that give the finish an aged patina, but you will cut through the old polish. Don't use this technique on valuable antiques and don't try it unless you are prepared to strip the old finish if reamalgamation doesn't work.

Sometimes it is obvious from the outset that repolishing alone will not be enough to repair a damaged finish. The dresser top shown in Illus. 6-7 is a good example. This finish is so badly damaged that most finishers would prob-

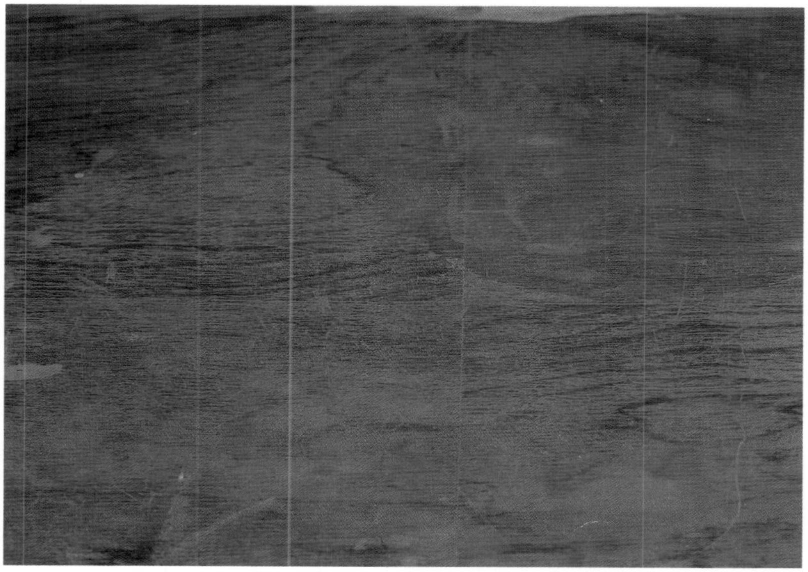

Illus. 6-7. This dresser top is so badly damaged that repolishing alone won't restore it. In a case such as this, you can try reamalgamating the old finish.

ably start by stripping off the old finish. Just to show how effective reamalgamation is, I describe and illustrate below, step by step, how this procedure will repair the top of the dresser.

Begin by adding a lot of alcohol to a rubber and rubbing the entire surface very hard. This will dissolve the top layer of old polish (Illus. 6-8). What you are trying to do when reamalgamating the finish is to dissolve the damaged layers of polish and work down to a smooth, undamaged layer of polish. In a severe case such the dresser top I'm working on, the finish may be damaged all the way down to the surface of the wood. Therefore, in that case, rub the surface with a synthetic finishing pad and a lot of alcohol (Illus. 6-9). Don't use steel wool for this operation because it will leave steel particles in the shellac.

Once you have a smooth surface, use a rubber to smooth

Illus. 6-8. The first step in reamalgamating the finish is to rub the surface with a rubber wet with alcohol.

Illus. 6-9. In severe cases, it may be necessary to use a synthetic finishing pad and lots of alcohol to dissolve the old polish.

out the dissolved shellac. Use very light pressure on the rubber. This step is very similar to fadding. Now, let the finish rest overnight. This method reuses most of the original shellac, so you have preserved the original color, although it has been redissolved and reapplied. The next day the surface will look about the same as if you had fadded it. It now needs to be smoothed and polished. If it is smooth but dull, you can begin applying more polish.

If it is lumpy or has ridges left from the rubber, then you will have to sand it smooth with 220-grit sandpaper (Illus. 6–10).

Now, apply fresh polish using the bodying technique (Illus. 6-11). When the original polish is made from a dark-colored shellac such as button lac or orange, the repolished surface may be lighter than it was originally because some of the original polish is absorbed into the rubber or sanded

Illus. 6-10. Let the reamalgamated finish dry, and then sand it with 220-grit sandpaper.

Illus. 6-11. After the surface has been sanded smooth, apply more polish following the directions given in Chapter Four for bodying.

off. If you want to darken the finish, use orange or garnet shellac for the repolishing. If you are happy with the present color, use blonde or white shellac. When you feel that the bodying is complete, proceed to the stiffing and spiriting-off stages exactly as described in Chapter Four.

When you are done, you have preserved the original look of the finish and reused much of the old materials. The finish won't look like new, but that's not what you intended. You want it to still show some stains and dents acquired with age that give it a patina (Illus. 6-12).

Illus. 6-12. Compare this photograph with Illus. 6-7, which shows the dresser top before reamalgamation. Reamalgamating the finish has restored the original color and given the surface an acceptable finish while still preserving some of the stains and marks that add to the patina.

CHAPTER SEVEN

Varnishes

ACCORDING TO LEGEND, the term varnish is derived from the name of the wife of King Ptolemy III of Egypt: Berenice. Queen Berenice was famed for her long, amber-colored hair. While her husband was at war with Syria, she made a vow that she would sacrifice her hair to the war god in return for the safety of Ptolemy. When her husband did return safely, Berenice cut off her hair and gave it as an offering of gratitude to the gods. According to the legend, the long tresses were taken up into the sky to become a constellation of stars. This constellation is still known today as Berenice's Hair (Coma Berenices).

The golden color of some natural resins such as amber and sandarac reminded the ancients of Berenice's golden hair, so they often referred to these resins as "bernice." Over time, the spelling changed to "vernice." By the 1500's, the name vernice referred to liquid finishing material made using these resins. The English word varnish is derived from "vernice."

Varnish is a term used to describe many different wood-finishing products. Over the years, it has at times been used to refer to almost any type of thick-bodied, transparent finishing product that produces a thick surface film on the wood. This material may or may not be called varnish, depending on how it is applied. For example, shellac is called polish when it is applied using the French-polishing method, but when it is brushed on, it has traditionally been called varnish.

In this chapter, I describe two general types of varnishes that have a long history in wood finishing: *spirit* and *oil* varnishes. There are many modern types of varnishes that contain synthetic resins. I will not discuss them in this book; if you want information on these products, refer to *Wood Finisher's Handbook* or *Finishing Basics*.

SPIRIT VARNISH

Spirit varnish is made from natural resins that are dissolved in alcohol. Shellac is the only spirit varnish that is commonly used today, but in previous times many different types of spirit varnish were available. Most of the time, a spirit varnish was made from several different ingredients. Spirit varnishes can be tough and beautiful, but they are not very water-resistant, and if alcohol is spilled on them, the finish will dissolve.

Before the development of modern finishing materials, spirit varnishes were favored when a very clear finish was

Illus. 7-1. Varnish provides a tough yet beautiful protective coat on wood.

Illus. 7-2. In the 1700's, spirit varnishes were preferred over oil varnishes. Oil varnishes of the day were dark amber in color and would obscure the details of the inlay work popular at the time. Spirit varnish could be made practically colorless, so the contrasting colors of the inlay would show through. This eagle inlay has been varnished with Roubo's white varnish. The formula for this varnish is given later in this chapter.

desired (Illus. 7-2). In most cases, spirit varnishes are "whiter" (more transparent and colorless) than oil varnishes. Some of the old formulas are difficult to work with, and the finishes produced can be brittle, as evidenced by the tiny hairline cracks seen on some antiques.

When you want the finish to look appropriate for the time period, but you aren't concerned with the historical accuracy of the ingredients, shellac is a good choice. Shellac is more durable and flexible than some of the other ingredients used in spirit varnish. Shellac is by far the best of the spirit varnish materials.

Stalker and Parker describe both a seed-lac varnish and a shellac varnish in their book *A Treatise of Japaning and Varnishing,* published in 1688 (Illus. 7-3). It is interesting to note that the process of mixing shellac has not changed since then. Even though shellac was known and used from an early date, it was not widely used before the 1800's, because the blonde and white grades were not available. Today, we may consider a deep-amber finish the mark of an antique, but, in the past, wood finishers were looking for a completely colorless finish. In many cases, they sacrificed qualities such as durability or flexibility in favor of a totally white finish. White or blonde shellac will have an appearance similar to the white spirit varnishes made using sandarac, but it is more durable and easier to work with.

Because the alcohol solvent evaporates quickly, spirit varnishes behave very differently from slow-drying oil varnishes. The fast drying time can be an advantage, because you can apply several coats in one day and there is less chance of dust contamination when the surface dries quickly. Allow at least six hours between coats.

It is advisable to thin the varnish to the consistency of two-pound-cut or three-pound-cut shellac. Apply spirit varnish with a soft-bristle brush. Apply the varnish in thin coats, working quickly. Once you have brushed on a coat, don't go back over the area again, because the varnish starts to dry immediately. Attempts to smooth out the finish by brushing it a second time will usually make it worse. Apply two coats of varnish the first day; then let the surface dry for two days.

Each new coat of spirit varnish slightly dissolves the previous coat, so the layers all fuse together. This means that it is not necessary to sand between coats to ensure good adhesion. You can sand between coats to remove rough spots, but, if the surface is smooth, you don't have to sand it. You will usually have to sand the finish after the second coat has been dry for two days. This will remove the roughness caused by raised wood fibres.

Before sandpaper was widely available, sand leathers, scouring rushes, or sharkskin would have been used. (See Chapter Two.) You can use 220-grit sandpaper. After sanding, apply two more coats and let the finish dry overnight. After applying two more coats, let the varnish dry for two days; then sand the surface again with 220-grit sandpaper. Finally, apply two more coats of varnish. This makes a total of eight coats.

Spirit-Varnish Ingredients

Spirit varnishes can be made from many different natural resins used individually or in different combinations (Illus. 7-4 and 7-5). Most of these ingredients are still available, but they will be difficult to find. I have purchased them by mail from several companies that specialize in finishing

A

TREATISE

OF

JAPANING

AND

VARNISHING

How to make VARNISHES.

To make Seed-Lacc-Varnish.

TAke one gallon of good spirit, and put it in as wide-mouthed a bottle as you can procure; for when you shall afterwards strain your varnish, the Gums in a narrow-mouthed bottle may stick together, and clog the mouth, so that it will be no easie task to separate or get them out. To your spirits add one pound and a half of the best Seed-lacc; let it stand the space of 24 hours, or longer, for the Gum will be the better dissolved: observe to shake it very well, and often, to keep the Gums from clogging or caking together. When it hath stood its time, take another bottle of the same bigness, or as many quart-ones as will contain your varnish; and your strainer of flannel made as aforesaid in this book, fasten it to a tenter-hook against a wall, or some other place convenient for straining it, in such a posture, that the end of your strainer may almost touch the bottom of your Tin-tunnel, which is supposed to be fixed in the mouth of your empty bottle, on purpose to receive your strained varnish. Then shake your varnish well together, and pour or decant into your strainer as much as conveniently it will hold, only be sure to leave room for your hand, with which you must squeeze out the varnish; and when the bag by so doing is almost drawn dry, repeat it, till your strainer being almost full of the dregs of the Gums, shall (the moisture being all pressed out) require to be discharged of them: which fæces or dregs are of no use, unless it be to burn, or fire your chimny. This operation must be continued, till all your varnish is after this manner strained; which done, commit it to your bottles close stopt, and let it remain undisturbed for two or three days: then into another clean empty bottle pour off very gently the top of your varnish, so long as you perceive it to run very clear, and no longer; for as soon as you observe it to come thick, and muddy, you must by all means desist: and again, give it time to rest and settle, which 'twill do in a day or two; after which time you may attempt to draw off more of your fine varnish, and having so done you may lay it up, till your art and work shall call for its assistance. Tis certain, that upon any emergency or urgent occasion you may make varnish in less time than 24 hours, and use it immediately, but the other I recommend as the best and more commendable way: besides, the varnish which you have from the top of the bottles first pour'd off, is of extraordinary use to adorn your work,

and render it glossy and beautiful. Some Artists, through hast or inadvertency, scruple not to strain their varnish by fire or candlelight: but certainly day-light is much more proper, and less dangerous; for should your varnish through negligence or chance take fire, value not that loss, but rather thank your stars that your self and work-house have escaped. Should I affirm, that the boiling the Lacker and Varnish by the fire, were prejudicial to the things themselves, I could easily make good the assertion; for they are as well and better made without that dangerous element, which if any after this caution will undertake, they may feelingly assure themselves that tis able to spoil both the Experiment and Operator. On the other hand, no advantage or excellence can accrue either to Lacker or Varnish; especially when, as some of them do, tis boiled to so great a height, that this Ætna is forc'd to throw out its fiery eruptions, which for certain consume the admiring Empedocles, who expires a foolish and a negligent Martyr; and it would almost excite ones pitty, to see a forward ingenious undertaker, perish thus in the beginning of his Enterprise; who might have justly promised to erect a noble and unimitable piece of Art, as a lasting monument of his fame and memory: but (unhappy man) his beginning and his end are of the same date; his hopes vanish, and his mischance shall be registered in doggrel Ballad, or be frightfully represented in a Puppet-shew, or on a Sign-post.

To make Shell-Lacc-varnish.

Whosoever designs a neat, glossy piece of work, must banish this as unserviceable for, and inconsistent with, the rarities of our Art. But because tis commonly used by those that imploy themselves in varnishing ordinary woods, as Olive, Walnut, and the like; tis requisite that we give you directions for the composition of it, that if your conveniency or fancy lead that way, you may be supplied with materials for the performance. Having therefore in readiness one gallon of the best Spirit, add to it one pound and a half of the best Shell-Lacc. This mixture being well stirred and shaked together, should stand about twenty four hours before tis strained: You might have observed, that the former varnish had much sediment and dregs; this on the contrary has none, for it wholly dissolves, and is by consequence free from all dross or fæces; tis requisite however to strain it, that the sticks and straws, which often are in the Gum, may by this percolation be separated from the varnish. But although this admits of no sediment, and in this case differs from the aforementioned varnish, yet tis much inferior also to it in another respect; That this will never be fine, clear, and transparent, and therefore 'twill be lost labour to endeavour, either by art or industry, to make it so. This small advantage however doth arise, that you need not expect or tarry for the time of its perfection,

Excerpt continues on page 64

Illus. 7-3. This excerpt from Stalker and Parker's *A Treatise of Japaning and Varnishing*, which continues on page 64, gives directions for preparing seed-lac and shellac spirit varnishes. The process hasn't changed much since this was written in 1688.

for the same minute that made it, made it fit for use. This, as I hinted before, is a fit varnish for ordinary work that requires not a polish; for though it may be polished, and look well for the present, yet like a handsome Ladies beautiful face, it hath no security against the injuries of time; for but a few days will reduce it to its native mist and dulness. Your common Varnish-dawbers frequently use it, for tis doubly advantageous to them: having a greater body than the Seed-Lacc, less labour and varnish goes to the perfecting their work; which they carelesly slubber over, and if it looks tolerably bright till tis sold, they matter not how dull it looks afterward; and lucre only being designed, if they can compass that, fa-rewel credit and admiration. Poor insufficient Pretenders, not able to make their work more apparent, or more lasting than their knavery! And tis pretty to think, that the same misty cloak will not cover the fraud and the impostor! that the first should be a foil to the second, and the dull foggy work serve only to set off the knavish Artist in his most lively colours! But to conclude, if with a pint of this varnish you mix two ounces or more of Venice-turpentine, it will harden well, and be a varnish good enough for the inside of Drawers, frames of Tables, Stan-pillars, frames of Chairs, Stools, or the like. Painters Lacker made also with this Varnish, and something a larger quantity of Turpentine put to it, serves very well for lackering of Coaches, Houses, Signs, or the like, and will gloss with very little heat, and, if occasion be, without.

products. Artists still use varnishes made from some of these ingredients. Small bottles of the liquid varnish are available from art-supply stores. I have applied the individual resins dissolved in alcohol to the birch sample shown in Illus. 7-6, so you can compare the color of each resin.

Resins are naturally produced by plants and trees. When a tree is injured, it exudes a liquid resin to cover the wound. On exposure to air, the resin hardens. Resins can be harvested either from naturally occurring wounds or by intentionally cutting into the bark of a tree or the stem of the plant and then letting the resins accumulate. Some types of resin form small tear-shaped drops; others are simply irregular lumps. The best-quality resins are harvested while they still cling to the tree or plant. If they have fallen to the ground before harvesting, they may have more dirt or impurities embedded in them.

Resins that are harvested from living trees and plants are called *recent resins. Fossil resins* are mined from deposits in the ground. They are the remnants of ancient forests. Fossil resins are generally harder than recent resins, because thousands of years of slow oxidation have chemically altered them.

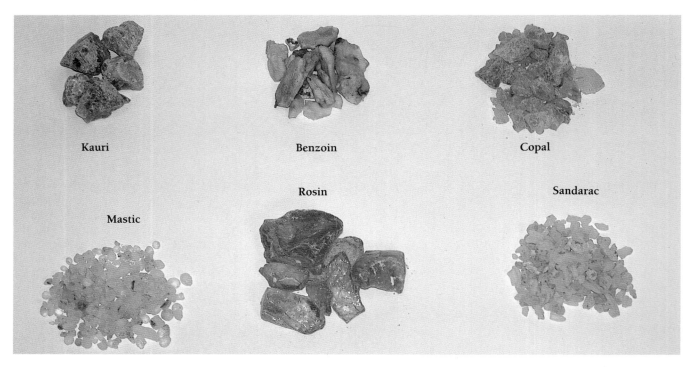

Illus. 7-4. Spirit varnishes are made from natural resins. Shown in the top row, from left to right, are kauri, benzoin, and copal. On the bottom row, from left to right, are mastic, rosin, and sandarac.

Illus. 7-5. Elemi (left) is added to spirit varnish to provide flexibility. Balsam (right) is added to give the varnish a high gloss.

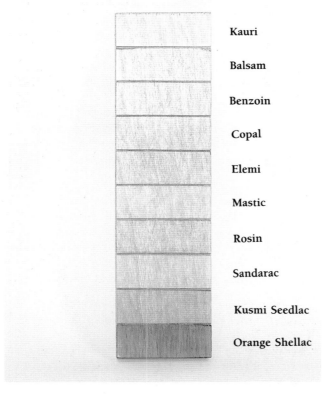

Kauri

Balsam

Benzoin

Copal

Elemi

Mastic

Rosin

Sandarac

Kusmi Seedlac

Orange Shellac

Illus. 7-6. I have dissolved each of the resins in alcohol and applied them to this birch sample so you can see the color of each. The resins shown, from top to bottom, are kauri, balsam, benzoin, copal, elemi, mastic, rosin, sandarac, Kusmi seed-lac, and orange shellac. During the 1700's, wood finishers wanted a colorless varnish. You can see why sandarac and mastic were the most popular resins at that time; they haven't changed the color of the birch at all. The rest of the resins add varying degrees of amber color to the wood.

Below is a description of the resins and other ingredients commonly used in spirit varnishes and their properties.

• *Alcohol* is the solvent used to dissolve the other ingredients in spirit varnish. In old formulas, it may be called *spirits of wine*.

The alcohol available to wood finishers in earlier days was often of unknown quality. It was usually distilled from wine or brandy, and it may have contained almost 50 percent water. Water causes the varnish to go cloudy, so it was important to determine the quality of the alcohol. The gunpowder method of testing alcohol has already been described in Chapter Three. The more-accurate hydrometer method was used in the 18th century by some finishers. A hydrometer is a sealed glass tube that is weighted at one end. It floats on the alcohol. The percentage of water in the alcohol will determine how high the tube floats. A graduated scale within the tube is read at the liquid level, giving an accurate measure of the water content of the alcohol.

Today, you can use denatured alcohol sold as shellac solvent to make spirit varnishes without worrying about water contamination.

• **Anime** is the archaic name for fossil copal resin. Fossil resins are mined from deposits in the ground. The resins accumulate at the site of an ancient forest. The fossil copal resins are virtually exhausted today. The original resin the word anime refers to—copal resin—is no longer available, but kauri resin from New Zealand is a reasonable substitute. Kauri resin is a superior resin that makes very good varnish. In the 1800's, kauri was an ingredient in most quality varnishes; it can be used in both spirit and oil varnish.

• **Balsam** is a resin collected from coniferous trees such as pine, fir, spruce, balsam, and larch. It was considered an inferior ingredient in varnish, but was used to give the varnish a high gloss. It may be referred to in old formulas as chian turpentine (derived from Mediterranean pines), Strasburg turpentine (derived from German fir trees), and Venice turpentine (derived from European larch trees).

Balsam should not be confused with modern turpentine. The product that is now called turpentine used to be called *turpentine oil* or *spirits of turpentine*. It is a liquid solvent made by distilling pine-tree sap.

The types of balsam most readily available today are copaiba balsam and Canadian balsam.

• **Benzoin** is a resin from the *styrax* benzoin tree that grows in tropical Asia. It was used in spirit varnishes of the 16th and 17th centuries. It has a pleasant odor that is still faintly recognizable on antiques. It is often added to classic varnishes to reproduce this characteristic smell. In old formulas, it may be called benjamin.

• **Copal** Several different resins have been called copal. Some types of copal can be mixed with oils to make an oil varnish. The copal varnish that is available at art-supply stores is an oil-based varnish.

The type of copal used in spirit varnish is called spirit or Manila copal. This is a resin harvested from trees in the *Agathis* genus. It is added to give toughness to the varnish.

• **Elemi** is a soft resin produced by trees in the Burseraceae family. It is added to varnish formulas to make the dried finish more elastic. It may be called allemy in old formulas. Elemi may be available at art-supply stores.

• **Gum Arabic** is a gum produced by trees in the *Acacia* genus. It is included in some old formulas for spirit varnish.

• **Lavender oil** is oil distilled from the lavender plant. It was first produced in the 1500's. It is very similar in characteristics to turpentine oil, except that turpentine oil will not mix with alcohol, while lavender oil will. It is used to make the spirit varnish easier to level or smooth so that brush marks flow out better. It may also be called *oil of spike* or *spike lavender*.

• **Mastic** is a soft resin that is very clear. It is a pale yellow color that may darken slightly with age. It was used when a light-colored varnish was desired. It is harvested from the *Pistacia lentiscus* tree that grows in the Mediterranean region. The best-quality mastic comes as small drop-shaped beads called "tears." These have been harvested while still attached to the tree. The lower grades of mastic have been harvested from the ground and may contain impurities. Mastic is sold at art-supply stores.

• **Rosin** is the resin left after balsam from trees such as pine, fir, spruce, balsam, and larch is distilled to make spirits of turpentine. Like balsam, it was considered an inferior ingredient in varnish. It gives the varnish a high gloss. It may be referred to in old formulas as colophony, when it was derived from American pine trees, or as Greek pitch, when it was derived from the Aleppo pine.

• **Sandarac** is a brittle resin. It is derived from Alerce trees (*Tetraclinus articulata*) that grow in the Atlas mountains of North Africa and Cypress pine trees (*Callistris quadrivalvis*). In old formulas, it may be called gum juniper. It was probably the most widely used resin for varnish-making, because it is very clear and dissolves easily in alcohol. Because sandarac used alone forms a very brittle film, elemi was often added to sandarac varnish to improve its flexibility.

Sandarac varnish starts out almost colorless, but with age it slowly becomes darker and reddish. The best-quality sandarac is harvested while still attached to the tree and is called "tears" of sandarac. Lower grades are harvested from the ground and may contain impurities. Sandarac varnish is still sold at art-supply stores.

• *Shellac* Shellac is unique among the natural resins because it is produced by an insect instead of a plant. A more complete discussion of shellac is given in Chapter Three. It produces a tough, flexible varnish.

Shellac varies in color, depending on the type of shellac used. Early varnish formulas used seed-lac, button lac, or orange shellac and the varnish had a dark orange or brown color. Seed-lac was considered the best type for use in spirit varnish in the 1600's, and it produced a lighter color of varnish than the orange shellac. In old formulas when gum lac is specified, kusmi seed-lac is probably referred to. When old formulas specify shellac, use orange shellac.

Lighter-colored types of shellac were not available until the late 1700's. Although shellac was used in a limited way for a long time, its dark color made it less desirable when finishers were striving for a light-colored varnish. After lighter forms of shellac became available, it soon became one of the most desirable ingredients in a spirit varnish.

Making Spirit Varnish

There are several formulas for spirit varnish that can be found in published materials from the 1600's onwards; unfortunately, probably the very best formulas were never published, because the finishers were very secretive about their personal methods. In this section, I give the formulas for four types of spirit varnish that are historically accurate and that I have personally tested (Illus. 7-7).

You will need a mortar and pestle to grind the resins and a scale to weigh the ingredients. Some of the ingredients will come as small lumps called tears or as large chunks; these will need to be ground to powder in the mortar and pestle (Illus. 7-8). Shellac flakes do not need to be ground. After powdering the ingredients in the mortar and pestle and mixing them, put the powder in a glass jar and fill the jar with alcohol. Shake up the ingredients and place the jar on the windowsill to be warmed by the sun. Some of the old formulas call for heating the mixture; since alcohol is highly flammable, I don't recommend this. The formulas presented here can be made without heating.

Agitate the mixture occasionally. When it is completely dissolved, let it settle for a day or two. Any undissolved particles and bits of dirt will settle to the bottom of the jar.

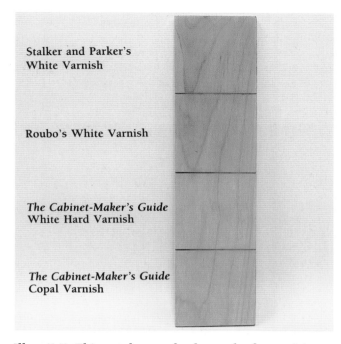

Stalker and Parker's White Varnish

Roubo's White Varnish

The Cabinet-Maker's Guide White Hard Varnish

The Cabinet-Maker's Guide Copal Varnish

Illus. 7-7. This maple sample shows the four spirit varnishes that I give formulas for in this chapter. From top to bottom, they are: Stalker and Parker's white varnish (1688), Roubo's white varnish (1769), *The Cabinet-Maker's Guide* white hard varnish (1825), and *The Cabinet-Maker's Guide* copal varnish (1825).

Illus. 7-8. Use a mortar and pestle to crush the resins to powder. This will make it easier to dissolve them in alcohol.

Now, pour the liquid into a clean container, leaving the sediment behind. Pouring the liquid through several layers of cloth was often recommended to further filter the varnish so that there would not be any undissolved particles that can lead to "seediness" or a rough texture (Illus. 7-9).

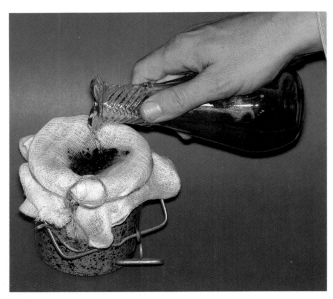

Illus. 7-9. Natural resins contain a lot of dirt. After the resins are completely dissolved in alcohol, strain the varnish through several layers of cloth to remove the impurities.

In the formulas below, liquids are measured in United States liquid measure quarts, pints, and fluid ounces; solids are measured in avoirdupois ounces and drams. A dram is one-sixteenth of an ounce.

Stalker and Parker's White Varnish

This formula is found in the book A *Treatise of Japaning and Varnishing,* published in 1688. The original formula made about a gallon of varnish. I have decreased the amounts so that about one quart of varnish can be made.

4 ounces of sandarac

4 drams of mastic

12 drams of Venice turpentine (balsam)

6 drams of copal

2 drams of elemi

2 drams of benzoin

2 drams of anime (use kauri as a substitute)

2 drams of rosin

12 ounces of alcohol

Roubo's White Varnish

This formula is based on one published around 1769 by André Jacques Roubo in his book *The Art of the Woodworker.* It is a very clear (white) varnish. Roubo recommends it for use on rosewood or holly because it won't alter the color of the wood.

5 ounces of sandarac

2 ounces of elemi

2 ounces of mastic

1 ounce of oil of lavender

1 pint of alcohol

The Cabinet-Maker's Guide White Hard Varnish

This formula comes from *The Cabinet-Maker's Guide.* It is a very clear varnish that is easy to make and use. The original formula made about two gallons. I have reduced the proportions so that approximately one quart can be made.

1 quart of alcohol

10 ounces of sandarac

2 ounces of mastic

½ ounce of anime (use kauri as a substitute)

The Cabinet-Maker's Guide Copal Varnish

This varnish from *The Cabinet-Maker's Guide* is probably the most durable of the four, but because it uses orange shellac, it has an amber color.

1 quart of alcohol

1 ounce of Manila copal

½ ounce of orange shellac

Changing Varnish

When a varnish was colored with a dye or pigment, it was called a "changing varnish"; today, we call it a "varnish stain." Changing varnishes were used to enhance or change the natural color of the wood. They were usually red or yellow (Illus. 7-10). Spirit varnish can be colored red or yellow by adding dragon's blood, sandalwood extract, yellowwood extract, or gamboge. (See Chapter Ten for details about these dyes.)

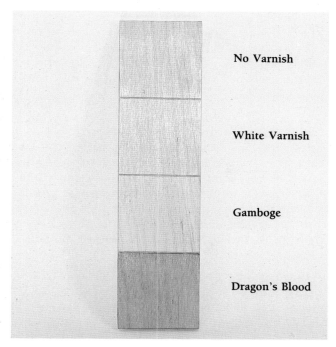

No Varnish

White Varnish

Gamboge

Dragon's Blood

Illus. 7-10. A changing varnish uses colored resins. On these maple pieces two types of changing varnishes are shown: dragon's blood added to white varnish, shown on the bottom, and gamboge added to white varnish, shown above it. Compare these changing varnishes to the top piece, which has no varnish, and to the white-varnish piece shown below.

OIL VARNISHES

Oil varnish has probably been in use longer than spirit varnish. It is made from drying oils such as linseed, poppyseed, or walnut oil. Natural resins added to the oil turn it into varnish. Many of the same resins used in spirit varnishes are also used in oil varnish.

Oil varnish is tougher and more water-resistant than spirit varnish. It has always been used in applications where these qualities were of overriding importance—shipbuilding, for example.

Just as today, the choice of finishing materials for furniture in the past was largely based on the current fashion. Sometimes a dark-colored varnish would be acceptable, and other times only a colorless spirit varnish would do. For centuries, wood finishers tried to develop a colorless varnish that would be tough and waterproof. This quest was finally realized in the 20th century with the development of synthetic resin varnishes.

Most of the modern synthetic varnishes are virtually colorless. This is not true of the classic oil varnishes; they range in color from light amber to dark brown. A classic oil varnish would be used today to duplicate the color of an antique finish or for its rubbing characteristics. Several modern finishes can be rubbed out using fine abrasives with good results, but the best rubbed finish still comes from a traditional rubbing varnish.

Oil varnish is difficult and dangerous to make, so it is fortunate that several manufacturers still sell traditional oil varnishes. These ready-made varnishes are suitable for virtually any project that requires an oil varnish. Only the most exacting museum-quality restoration work will require specially mixed oil varnish.

Many old-time varnish makers were seriously injured or killed making oil varnish. This is because some of the resins are only partially soluble in oil, that is, they sometimes needed to be dissolved in a solvent such as spirits of turpentine first. Most of the ingredients would not mix together unless the varnish was cooked. The hazards involved in heating a mixture of highly flammable materials are obvious!

Most common oil varnishes in the 1700's were made from boiled linseed oil and rosin (colophony), with small quantities of other resins. The resulting varnish was dark brown and too soft to be rubbed out with abrasives.

The Martin family were varnish makers in France during the 1700's. They had the reputation for making the highest-quality oil varnishes. They developed an oil varnish that was lighter in color and hard enough to be rubbed to a high gloss with fine-abrasive powders. This varnish was clear and tough when first applied, but it hasn't stood the test of time as well as the spirit varnishes. The high temperature needed to mix the resins with the oil caused the resins to chemically break down, allowing the varnish to deteriorate more rapidly than the spirit varnishes. Any surviving furniture originally finished with this type of varnish has probably been refinished with a more durable finishing material.

Amber is an important resin used in oil varnishes. Amber is not completely soluble in alcohol, so it was not used in spirit varnishes but it was widely used in the best-quality oil varnishes. Amber is a fossil resin of prehistoric forests of white cedar and arborvitae. It is found in the region around the Baltic Sea. It is usually mined from beds (a geological layer), but some amber is collected along the seashore where it has washed up after being eroded from the earth. The sea amber is polished and clean-looking, but it doesn't make as good a varnish as the mined amber. The amber from the earth is covered with a brown crust.

Making amber varnish was complicated and dangerous.

Here is a description of the process for historical interest. The first step in making amber varnish is called "running the resin." A melting pot is placed on a fire until it reaches 300 degrees Fahrenheit or more; then some chian or cyprus turpentine (balsam) is put into the pot to melt.

When the turpentine is fluid, crushed amber is added and cooked for 15 minutes. The pot is then removed from the fire and copal resin that has been crushed into small pieces is added, along with more chian turpentine. The mixture is then stirred while spirits of turpentine is added. When the resins and turpentine oil have been mixed together well, the covered pot is placed on a hot fire for 30 minutes. This ends the running-the-resin step.

Next, the pot is removed from the fire and some colophony (rosin) is stirred in. The pot is then covered and placed on the fire again to cook until all of the resins are dissolved. Then the pot is again removed from the fire and, after the mixture cools a little, the oil is poured in. Linseed, poppy, or walnut oil could be used. The oil used during the 1700's was what we would call boiled oil today; it was treated with driers so that it would dry more quickly than raw oil. The oil had to be boiling hot. It was added a little at a time and stirred in briskly.

The oil and resin mixture is placed on the fire again until it begins to boil. In the meantime, some turpentine is heated on a second fire. When the varnish begins to boil, the pot is removed from the fire (the original formula says to take it some distance away from the fire, to avoid an explosion no doubt!), and the hot turpentine is poured in. The pot is placed again on the fire and allowed to boil; then it is removed and another pint of hot turpentine added. If everything has gone well, the varnish is now complete.

Amber varnish was much thinner than the oil varnishes we are accustomed to today. It took many coats to build up a usable film thickness. In many ways, it was almost like applying a heavy-bodied oil finish. First, six coats were brushed on; each coat was forced-dry by placing it in a room heated with stoves. When the sixth coat was dry, the finish was smoothed by rubbing with a wet rag and powdered pumice. After all traces of the pumice were removed, 12 more coats were brushed on and dried. Now, the varnish was ready to be rubbed out with pumice and rottenstone.

Driers

When looking through old varnish formulas, you may find suggestions to add ground glass to the varnish. The glass of the day had a high lead content; adding ground glass made the varnish dry harder, because the lead in the glass acted as a drier. A drier is a chemical compound that acts as a catalyst to speed up the oxidation reaction of drying oils. Lead was often used in the past. Today, we know that lead is highly poisonous and the use of lead as a drier has been discontinued. Other driers used in the past included burnt alum, burnt horn, garlic, and bone.

Types of Oil Varnish

By the mid 1800's, varnish makers were using more suitable resins such as dammar and kauri; this, along with better manufacturing methods, produced truly durable water-resistant varnishes. The natural-resin oil varnishes available today are similar to these 19th-century varnishes. They are divided into three classifications based on the proportions of oil and resin: long oil varnish, medium oil varnish, and short oil varnish.

• *Long Oil Varnish* Long oil varnish contains 40 to 100 gallons of oil for every 100 pounds of resin. The varnish film is tough and elastic. It is very water-resistant. Spar varnish falls into the category of long oil varnishes. It is designed for marine use. Exterior varnishes are always long oil varnished.

Tung oil became available in the United States after 1890; it is often used in long oil varnish because it adds to its water resistance. Long oil varnish is not suitable for use on furniture, because the film is too soft to be polished. Also, its drying time is very long, so there is an increased chance of dust getting into the finish.

• *Medium Oil Varnish* Varnish that contains 12 to 40 gallons of oil for every 100 pounds of resin is classified as a medium oil varnish. Medium oil varnish is often used for floor varnish. It dries faster and the film is harder than a long oil varnish, but it is more elastic and water-resistant than a short oil varnish. Medium oil varnish has some limited application in furniture finishing, but most furniture varnish is the short-oil type.

• *Short Oil Varnish* A short oil varnish only uses 5 to 12 gallons of oil for every 100 pounds of resin. The film is very hard and somewhat brittle. It is not as water-resistant as the varnishes that contain more oil. The main advantage of a short oil varnish is that it can be polished to a high gloss. Short oil varnish that is sold today is often labelled "rubbing varnish" or "tabletop varnish." Sometimes it is called "restoration varnish," because its natural oils and resins make it suitable for restoring antiques.

Applying Oil Varnish

The technique for applying an oil varnish is very different

from that used for spirit varnish. Whereas the spirit varnish must be applied quickly and not worked over once applied, oil varnish can be applied slowly and the wet varnish can be brushed out several times if necessary to produce a smooth application.

• **Filler** Open-grained woods will have to be filled if you want a glassy-smooth varnish surface. Even closed-grained woods can use a sealer coat. If you have stained the wood, apply a coat of one-pound-cut shellac before you apply the filler. This will protect the stain while you apply the filler.

A sealer coat of shellac is also useful on closed-grained woods; sometimes this sealer coat is called "liquid filler." It seals the wood so that the varnish will be absorbed equally over the entire surface. Without a sealer coat, the first coat or two of varnish will soak into the wood in some areas where the grain is especially absorbant; end grain and knots are particularly absorbant, but changes in the grain pattern can also cause some areas to absorb more than others. Areas where the varnish is absorbed will show up as dull spots called "sleepy patches." These sleepy patches won't have as thick of a film buildup as surrounding areas, so, even after a second coat, they will show up as depressions in the surface.

Plaster colored with stain was often used in England as a filler for open-grained wood, but the stains used faded, leaving a white or grey filler visible in the pores of the wood. Plaster filler is applied using the same technique described in Chapter Four.

You can use any of the commercially available fillers under varnish with good results. These fillers are a mixture of a fine mineral powder and oil. Follow the manufacturer's directions for the exact procedure. Usually, the filler comes in a concentrated form. It must be thinned before application. Brush on the thinned filler. When it is first applied, it will have a wet, glossy look. Let the filler sit on the wood until the gloss disappears. This may take from 15 minutes to half an hour. Don't let the filler stay on the wood so long that it begins to harden.

Now, wipe off the filler from the wood surface with a coarse cloth. Burlap works well, because the open weave will hold a lot of filler in the rag. At first, wipe the filler in a circular motion, to push it deep into the pores. When most of the filler has been removed from the wood surface, lightly wipe the surface with the grain to remove the remaining filler. Don't rub so hard that you pull the filler out of the pores.

Let the filler dry overnight: then wipe the surface with a clean cloth. If excess filler remains on the surface, it can be removed with 000 steel wool.

One of the best ways to fill the grain is to use the varnish as a filler, but the process involves more hand labor. Apply two coats of varnish to the wood and let them dry thoroughly; then use a hand scraper to scrape off all of the varnish on the wood surface. (See Chapter Two for details about hand scrapers.) All that will remain is the varnish that has seeped into the pores. The scraper will make this varnish level with the surrounding wood, leaving a flat, smooth ground for the next coat of varnish.

It is important that the filler coats be allowed to dry completely before scraping, because if they are still soft, the scraper may pull the varnish out of the pores. Also, if the varnish is not completely dry before you scrape it level with the surface, the varnish in the pores may shrink, leaving the pores visible on the surface. After the surface has been scraped smooth, you can start applying additional coats of varnish.

• **Brushing Technique** The surface quality of the final finish depends to a large degree on your skill with a brush. Use a high-quality bristle brush. A 2½-inch brush can be used for small work; a 4-inch brush is about as large a brush as you will ever need for large work.

Choose a well-ventilated, dust-free place to work. Varnish will remain tacky for several hours, so dust that settles on the surface will get trapped in the finish. If moisture from the air condenses on the surface before the film hardens, it will cause a problem called "bloom." Bloom is a cloudy white haze in the varnish film. Bloom was a greater problem in the past when the finisher had to work in a shop heated only by a wood-burning stove. If you are working under similar conditions, you should take the same precautions that the old finishers did. Apply varnish early in the day; this way, it can dry during the warmest part of the day, and it will be sufficiently dry before the temperature drops at night. Don't apply varnish on very humid days. A rainy day is actually better than a fair but humid day, because when it is raining, the moisture in the air is being released as rain instead of being trapped as vapor that can condense on the varnish. Of course, if you are working in a centrally heated and air-conditioned shop, none of these precautions are necessary.

Varnish should be applied in a warm environment: a temperature of 70 to 80 degrees Fahrenheit is best. At this temperature, the varnish will flow and can be levelled properly. If the temperature is below 60 degrees Fahrenheit, the varnish will be too thick to flow out and brush marks will become a problem. Varnishes available today are designed to be used as they come, with no further thinning necessary.

The surface to be varnished must be perfectly free from dust and grit. Just before you apply the varnish, wipe the surface with a tack cloth. This is a piece of cheesecloth that is treated with a sticky material. It will pick up the last traces of dust and grit.

Incidentally, when you look through old books on wood finishing, you may encounter instructions for making a tack cloth by moistening a rag with varnish and then letting it partially dry. *Don't do it!* This can be a very serious fire hazard. Any rag that has drying oil of the type found in wood-finishing products must be disposed of in an airtight, water-filled container. If you leave an oily rag around your shop, it can ignite unexpectedly because of the process called *spontaneous combustion*. The oil generates heat through a chemical process; as it dries under certain conditions, the heat can be great enough to start a fire. So just buy a commercially made tack cloth; they are made of materials that won't cause spontaneous combustion.

It will be easier to load the brush with varnish if you pour the varnish into a small bucket or an earthenware pot. Fill the bucket about halfway; this provides room at the top of the bucket to remove the excess varnish from the brush. The bucket doesn't have a lip like the original can has; the lip makes it difficult to properly load the brush.

In the past, varnishers used glazed earthenware pots to hold the varnish. These are still very good, because they don't have any seams or ridges. The smooth sides make it easy to pat off the brush, and they are easy to clean after use.

Load the brush by dipping it into the varnish about two-thirds of the way up the bristles. Don't dip it all the way up to the metal ferrule. As you remove the brush from the bucket, pat it gently against the side of the bucket. This will remove the excess varnish that is clinging to the outside of the brush, leaving only the interior of the brush loaded.

Patting the brush against the side is preferable to wiping it across the lip of a can. Wiping the brush on the lip can cause varnish to drop off the brush into the varnish in the can; this can cause bubbles in the varnish. Try to avoid creating bubbles in the can, because they can cling to the brush and show up on the surface of the wood. If bubbles are allowed to remain on the surface until it dries, they will form small craters.

The first step in brushing on a varnish is called "flowing on the varnish." Start brushing in the middle of the work and brush off its ends. Work in overlapping strokes towards the edges. This technique prevents varnish buildup and drips at the ends and edges. If you start at the end of the board, the brush must wipe across the arris. This will wipe the varnish off the brush and let it drip onto the end of the board. Cover the entire surface with a coat of varnish using this brushing technique.

The amount of varnish to use is also important. You want a coat that is heavy enough to flow out, but not so thick that it will run or sag. You can apply a slightly heavier coat to a horizontal surface. Vertical surfaces should be given a thinner coat, so the varnish won't sag or run.

When in doubt, it is better to apply a coat that is too thin. A thin coat may show a few brush marks, but they are easier to sand out than sags or runs. If the coat is too heavy, it can also wrinkle as it dries. The perfect coat will be thick enough that all of the brush marks flow out before the varnish begins to dry and yet no sags or runs appear. With a little experience, you should be able to judge how much varnish to apply by watching how it flows out.

Always be on the lookout for defects in the application as you work; they are much easier to correct while the varnish is wet. In fact, one of the advantages of varnish is that its slow drying time makes it possible to brush over the surface several times if necessary to eliminate sags or runs. If you let them dry, they are hard to correct. Sags and runs stay gummy in the area between the varnish and wood long after the varnish has dried. If you try to sand them off, you end up with a gummy, rough area.

The next step in brushing on varnish is called "brushing out." After the surface is completely covered with varnish, brush over the surface in long, even strokes. Don't add any varnish to the brush; here you want to smooth the varnish that is already on the surface. Some finishers like to brush out once across the grain and then finish by brushing out with the grain. This technique is useful if you applied too much varnish in one area, because it helps to distribute the varnish over the entire surface. If you have applied the varnish uniformly, it is better to always brush with the grain, because there is always the chance that some of the cross-grain brush strokes will show.

Examine the surface by letting light reflect off it. This way, you can detect any areas that were not coated completely; these areas are called "holidays." Brush over the holidays, applying more varnish if necessary to cover them with the same thickness of varnish as the rest of the surface. It may be necessary to brush out the entire surface again after you have recoated a holiday.

The final step is called "tipping off." Pat the brush against the side of the bucket to remove any excess varnish that you picked up during the brushing out. Now, hold the brush vertical and let the tips of the bristles just touch the surface. Lightly move the brush in straight strokes with the grain. Overlap each stroke. Here you want to give the coat its final smooth surface, so watch carefully as you tip off. If you see a problem in the finish, now is the time to correct it. After about 15 minutes, carefully examine the work. If you find some drips or runs, carefully brush them out.

After the first coat is dry, apply a second coat. When the second coat is dry, it is time to smooth out the surface and remove any dust nibs. Nowadays, the preferred method is to use 320-grit wet or dry sandpaper lubricated with water. Use a rubber sanding block. Sprinkle a little water on the surface and sand with the grain. As the surface dries, add a little more water. You don't want to flood the wood with water, because some may seep into it. Occasionally wipe the varnish dry with a rag and examine the surface; when it looks uniformly dull and all of the brush marks, dust nibs, bubble craters, and other imperfections have been sanded out, you can stop.

Varnishers in earlier times didn't have wet or dry sandpaper; they used a block of felt and powdered pumice for this operation. This process is called "felting down the varnish." Water is used as a lubricant. Don't use oil as a lubricant when felting down between coats; the residual oil can cause problems with the next coat. Begin by wiping a damp sponge over the surface. The felt should be soaked in water before use, then "charge" the felt by dipping it in some pumice. Now, rub the felt block over the varnish in a straight stroke with the grain.

After felting down the varnish, apply at least two more coats. If you plan on rubbing out the varnish, six coats will be better than four. Felt down the varnish again after the fourth coat and apply two more coats; then give it the final rubout.

- **Rubbing Out Varnish** For a truly fine varnished finish, the final surface should be rubbed out (Illus. 7-11). Rubbing out the finish makes it flat and removes the last traces of dust. The rubbing can also be used to produce the desired gloss from satin to high gloss. The rubbed-out satin finish has become popular fairly recently. In earlier times, varnish was always polished to a high gloss. The satin effect we see on antiques is the result of years of wear dulling the gloss.

The traditional way to rub out a finish uses natural abrasive powders such as pumice, rottenstone, and tripoli (Illus. 7-12). Today, there are many other abrasives that can be used for rubbing out a finish. Wet or dry sandpaper is often used for the initial flattening; finishers usually start with 400-grit sandpaper and then switch to 600 grit. The process can even be taken further with 1200-grit sandpaper. The new micro-abrasive papers are capable of completing the process, providing as high a gloss as is obtainable with the traditional rottenstone. In this book, I will confine my discussion to the traditional technique.

Pumice is a mineral abrasive that is volcanic in origin. It has been used as an abrasive in wood finishing for centuries. In the past, blocks of solid pumice were used to

Illus. 7-11. Rubbed-out varnish is a traditional favorite for tabletops. Notice how the reflected light reveals the perfectly smooth glossy surface.

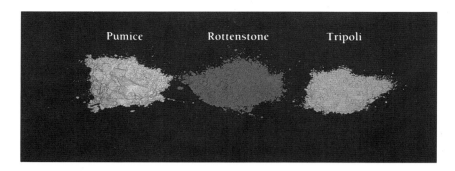

Illus. 7-12. Traditionally, natural abrasives are used to rub out varnish. Shown from left to right are pumice, rottenstone, and tripoli.

smooth wood in the same way we use sandpaper on a sanding block today. Powdered pumice is graded according to the size of its particles; No. 1 is coarse, No. 0 is average, F is fine, FF is extra fine, FFF is extra extra fine. The FF and FFF grades are usually used for rubbing varnish.

The first step in rubbing varnish is the same felting down process described earlier. Make sure that the varnish is completely hard; allow at least two days' drying time, although a week is better. The felt used should be at least ¼ inch thick. Wood-finishing supply stores still sell this type of felt. You can also get 1-inch-thick felt that makes a good block that is easy to hold. If you use the ¼-inch-thick felt, it will be easier to use if you make a wood-block handle for the felt. Use a damp-felt block with pumice powder on its face. If you store the pumice in a flat box such as a cigar box, you can press the damp face of the felt into the pumice to charge it. For this step, use extra-fine (FF) pumice. Add a little soap to a pan of water and wipe the soapy water onto the surface with a damp sponge.

Now, felt down the surface with the pumice (Illus. 7-13). Work over the entire surface uniformly. Don't rub too long in one spot. If you rub too hard or long in one place, it is possible to generate enough heat to soften the varnish. If this happens, the job will be ruined because the pumice will get imbedded in the soft varnish.

As you rub, look at the face of the felt occasionally. If little spots of varnish are building up on the felt, remove them and add a little more water. If you let these spots of caked-on varnish get large, they will scratch the finish.

Be careful near the edges; it is easy to rub through the varnish at the arrises. Mouldings and other details are difficult to rub. For these details, don't use the flat felt; use a soft rag and very little pressure.

Felt down the surface until it is uniformly dull and there are no visible defects. Don't rub any more than is necessary, because you are removing a little layer of varnish each time you do so. Now, wipe the surface dry with a clean rag. At this point, the finish will have a nice satin

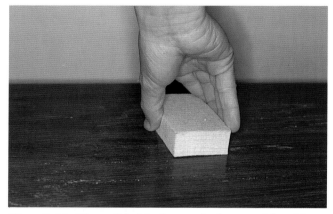

Illus. 7-13. Use a felt block to rub the varnish with pumice.

gloss; if you want this type of finish, you can stop. Traditionally, the finish should be polished to a higher gloss.

The next step is called "fine rubbing" or "oil rubbing." Use the extra-extra-fine (FFF) grade of pumice for this step. You can use soapy water for this step also, but it makes the pumice cut faster; the preferred method is to use oil as the lubricant. Raw linseed oil, olive oil, or paraffin oil can be used. Wipe a thin film of it on the surface of the work. Soak the felt in the oil; then charge the felt with pumice by dipping it into some.

Now, rub over the surface with long, straight strokes with the grain. At this stage, you are not trying to flatten or remove defects; all of that should have been accomplished in the last step. All you are trying to do is polish out the fine scratches left by the coarser grade of pumice. Once the surface looks uniformly polished, you can stop.

Rottenstone is a form of limestone. It is finer than pumice, so it is used to give the finish a high gloss. Tripoli is another fine abrasive that can also be used to polish the finish. To polish the finish with rottenstone, fold a piece of soft cloth into a square pad. Moisten the pad and sprinkle rottenstone on the face. Wipe the varnish with a sponge damp with soapy water; then polish the varnish using either a straight-line motion with the grain or a circular motion.

Add rottenstone as necessary during the first stages of the polishing; but as you get closer to a high gloss, don't add any more. The rottenstone will break into finer particles as you rub, so the abrasive will become progressively finer as the rubbing continues. Keep polishing until you reach the degree of gloss desired.

Wipe the finish dry, and then buff it with a clean, dry cloth. Rub vigorously to generate some heat from friction. This will partially soften the finish and smooth off the microscopic points left on the fine scratches that the rottenstone made.

The ''buffing step'' is where the difference between a natural-resin varnish and a synthetic varnish is really revealed. A synthetic-resin varnish such as polyurethane is so hard and heat-resistant that the microscopic scratches left by the finest abrasive will remain sharp no matter how hard you buff. This leaves a surface that looks great from some angles, but when the light hits it from a low angle, there appears to be a bluish haze on it. This is caused by the scratches acting like tiny prisms breaking up the light.

Buffing a natural-resin varnish will soften the resins slightly, due to the heat from friction. This will melt the sharp point off the scratch, leaving a glassy-smooth surface that reflects light beautifully with no haze.

CHAPTER EIGHT

Oil Finishes

NATURAL OILS HAVE been used as wood finishes since around the time of the ancient Egyptians. The oils used are derived from plants. The most useful oils are called "drying oils" (Illus. 8-1). When used alone, drying oils provide a penetrating finish that soaks into the wood.

Drying oils are also used in combination with other ingredients to make various types of finishing products. When resins are added to oils, a varnish is the result. When pigments are added to oils, then the material is called paint.

This chapter covers the use of oils as a penetrating finish. Penetrating finishes have several desirable characteristics. Because they soak into the wood, they help to strengthen the wood at the surface. Since the finish extends below the surface of the wood, shallow scratches and abrasions will not completely remove the protective finish as they might with a surface-film type of finish, and they are easy to apply.

The chemical process which causes drying oils to harden is called "oxidation." This is different from "evaporation." Solvent-based finishing products dry by evaporation. Shellac is a good example of evaporative drying. Alcohol is the solvent; it evaporates upon exposure

to air, leaving only the shellac resin on the surface of the wood.

When an oil dries by oxidation, a chemical process causes oxygen from the surrounding air to be drawn into the oil and to unite with it. Oxidation is much slower than evaporation. As the oxygen unites with the oil molecules, it causes the molecules to link together into long chains. This process is called "polymerization." Polymerization is the same process used to make modern plastics. When a drying oil hardens, it becomes a natural polymer with many of the same properties as modern plastics.

In its raw state, an oil dries very slowly. Driers added to the oil can speed up this process. In the past, lead was often used as a drier in oil. Lead has proven to be a dangerous health hazard, so today other types of driers are used.

Heating the oil will also speed up the drying process. Boiling the oil causes the polymerization process to begin; this will cause the oil to thicken. The oil is then cooled and placed in an airtight container. When the oil is applied to the wood and exposed to air, it will resume the polymerization process at the point it left off when it cooled.

In old instructions, oil that has been boiled or has had

Illus. 8-1. Drying oils have been used for centuries as wood finishes. Shown here are four types of oil that are discussed in this chapter. From left to right, they are walnut, linseed, red, and brown oil.

Walnut Oil   Linseed Oil   Red Oil   Brown Oil

driers added to it is often called "oil made drying." Today, it is usually called boiled or cooked oil.

Penetrating oils are thin-bodied. They will soak completely into the wood, leaving no measurable surface film. This results in a flat or satin sheen. Drying oils can be used to produce a gloss or semi-gloss finish, if they are thickened to the point that they will build a thin film on the surface. If the cooking process is continued long enough, the oil will thicken sufficiently to produce a glossy finish.

TYPES OF OIL

There are many types of oil that can be used in wood finishing. For most of the history of wood finishing, only three types were widely used: linseed, walnut, and poppyseed oil. Many other oils have been brought into widespread use since the beginning of the 20th century. Most of them are derived from the seed or nut of a plant or tree. The oil can be removed by cold-pressing, hot-pressing, or chemical processes.

Cold-pressing is the oldest way to extract the oil. The seeds or nuts are placed in a press and squeezed until the oil flows out of small holes in the press. Cold-pressing leaves quite a bit of the oil still trapped in the seeds or nuts, so more efficient methods are usually used.

Hot-pressing removes more of the oil by heating the seeds as they are being pressed. However, the most efficient method of removing the oil is the chemical process. Most of the oil produced today is extracted using chemicals such as sodium hydroxide, sodium carbonate, or sulfuric acid.

Cold-pressed linseed oil has not been available in large quantities since the 1930's. It is available in small quantities from art-supply stores. Some people believe that the cold-pressed oil is superior to chemically extracted oil.

Not all oils are drying oils. Nondrying oils such as olive, castor, almond, and mineral oil will remain liquid after prolonged exposure to air. Nondrying oil can be applied to wood; it soaks into the wood and offers some protection, but it will never harden.

Linseed Oil

Linseed oil is a drying oil derived from the seeds of the flax plant. Flax also produces the fibre used to make linen. The name linseed oil is a shortened version of linen-seed oil.

The first use of linseed oil is hard to determine. Evidence from Egyptian tombs suggests that the ancient Egyptians did not use linseed oil. Other ancient civilizations used linseed oil for medicinal purposes, but there is not enough evidence to determine if they used it as a wood finish. It was, however, definitely one of the major ingredients used in wood finishes by the 1600's. Linseed oil is mentioned by Stalker and Parker in the 1688 book *A Treatise of Japaning and Varnishing*.

Linseed oil is amber-colored and its color darkens with age, even after application. This property was often considered undesirable when light woods were in fashion, so other lighter-colored oils were substituted. Linseed oil was one of the most durable and water-resistant finishing products available to finishers prior to the introduction of tung oil. When its dark color was not a problem, linseed oil was widely used. Most furniture made from dark-colored wood was probably finished with linseed oil prior to the mid 1700's. The use of linseed-oil finishes remained popular even after the introduction of other oils and varnishes.

Raw linseed oil is often used as a lubricant in the French-polishing process. Boiled linseed oil is the type most often used for penetrating finishes. Modern boiled linseed oil contains metallic salts that act as driers to speed up the process of polymerization. When the oil is polymerized, it is tough but still elastic. This property allows the finish to stretch with the wood as seasonal changes in humidity cause the wood to shrink or swell. After many years, the polymerized linseed oil undergoes a chemical change that causes embrittlement. This means that it is no longer elastic. In a penetrating finish, embrittlement doesn't have much effect, but when linseed oil is used in a film-producing finish such as varnish or paint, embrittlement leads to tiny cracks in the finish.

Walnut Oil

Walnut oil was probably the first drying oil used as a wood finish. It may have been used as early as 100 AD. In medieval times, it was used to make varnish. It was definitely being used by the time of the Renaissance.

Walnut oil is often simply called nut oil; it comes from the nuts of the Persian walnut tree (*Juglans regia*). Cold-pressed walnut oil is very light in color, and it doesn't yellow with age. This property made walnut oil a favorite of wood finishers who were searching for a very clear finish to use on light-colored woods. When hot-pressed, the oil is greenish in color.

Walnut oil dries more slowly than linseed oil. Dried walnut oil will remain elastic for a long period of time before embrittlement causes cracking. Liquid walnut oil that is stored for a long time may become rancid.

Poppyseed Oil

Poppyseed oil comes from the seeds of the opium poppy. Poppyseed oil was used in the 1700's because of its pale color. Poppyseed oil doesn't dry as well as linseed oil. It may resoften after drying, especially in the presence of heat. Poppyseed oil also has more of a tendency to crack. The main reason poppyseed oil was used was because it was light in color and didn't yellow or darken with age; in all other respects, it is inferior to linseed oil.

Tung Oil

Tung oil is also called China-wood oil or China nut oil. It is the product of the nuts of the tung tree. The tree is native to China and it has been cultivated there and in surrounding areas for centuries. It has been used in China for many years. It was first exported to the United States in the 1890's. Soon it was in such great demand that shortages developed. The supply of tung oil in the United States did not fully meet the demand until commercial tung tree farms were planted in Florida in the 1920's.

Tung oil probably has the most desirable characteristics of all of the drying oils. Since its widespread introduction, it has rapidly overtaken linseed as the most useful oil in finishing furniture. The oil is amber in color and it will darken with age, so it is not suitable when a colorless oil is needed; but for all other applications, it is a superior oil. It is very tough, elastic, and water-resistant. The tung-oil finish will be resistant to alcohol, mild acids, and acetone.

Raw tung oil dries very slowly, but it will penetrate deeply into the wood and eventually harden. It can be used as a wood finish, but usually a mixture of raw tung oil, cooked oil, and thinners are used. Cooked oil is tung oil that has been heated. The heating process thickens the oil by stimulating the polymerization process. Cooked oil can be used to build a film on the surface and produce a high gloss. Various tung-oil products are sold for different purposes; the main difference between these products is the percentage of cooked oil in the formula.

A pure tung-oil finish consists of mostly raw tung oil with a little thinner added. There is no cooked oil in it. It is often preferred by experienced finishers. It dries slowly and is more difficult to apply than some of the other types of tung-oil products described below, but it can produce a high-quality finish.

Tung-oil sealer is a very thin oil that may contain about 20 percent cooked oil. It is used to achieve deep penetration below the wood surface before heavier-bodied oils are used.

Low-lustre tung oil produces a finish that has virtually no gloss. It contains about 25 percent cooked oil. This type of oil is very easy to apply, and it penetrates deeply into the wood. Additional coats of oil will increase the durability of the finish, but they will not build to a gloss.

Medium-lustre tung oil contains about 35 percent cooked oil. It will build to a satin gloss after several coats have been applied. Additional coats will increase the gloss. A medium-lustre oil produces a hard surface, but it doesn't penetrate as deeply as the low-lustre finish. When deep penetration is desired, the first coats can be a tung-oil sealer or low-lustre oil.

High-gloss tung oil contains over 50 percent cooked oil. It will quickly build to a high gloss, but it takes more skill to apply than the other types. It must be applied quickly because it will begin to gel soon after being applied. If the surface is rubbed after the oil gets tacky, lap marks will be visible in the finish.

Safflower Oil

Safflower oil is derived from the seeds of the safflower plant, which is native to Asia. It wasn't used in the United States until 1949.

Sunflower Oil

Sunflower oil is derived from sunflower seeds. It is a pale yellow drying oil. When dry, it is softer and gummier than linseed oil.

Soybean Oil

Soybean oil is pressed from soybeans. It has a pale color and does not turn yellow, but it is slow-drying and doesn't dry as hard as linseed oil.

Perilla Oil

Perilla oil is produced by the seeds of the *Perilla ocimoides* plant, which grows in China, Japan, and the surrounding area. Perilla oil is very similar to linseed oil, but it dries more quickly.

Oiticica Oil

Oiticica oil is produced by the *Licania rigida* tree, which grows in Brazil. It is similar to tung oil in appearance and properties.

APPLYING AN OIL FINISH

The directions given here are for a linseed-oil finish, but they generally apply to any type of oil.

You will have many oily rags after you have applied an oil finish. These can be a fire hazard unless you dispose of them properly. The safest way is to place them in a metal container that is filled with water and has a lid. Oily rags left in a pile or placed in a trash bin can burst into flames unexpectedly due to a process called spontaneous combustion.

Surface preparation is very important when an oil finish is used. A penetrating oil finish will never be any smoother than the surface of the wood, because there is no film on top of the wood to fill in small scratches. Prepare the wood by planing and scraping, and then sand it with fine sandpaper. For most finishes, I stop sanding with 220-grit sandpaper on the bare wood, but for a penetrating finish I use up to 320-grit sandpaper.

You can use either raw or boiled linseed oil for this finish. Raw linseed oil does eventually dry; it just dries more slowly than the boiled oil. Traditionally, raw linseed oil has the reputation of producing a harder finish than the boiled oil, but its drying time is unpredictable; sometimes it will remain tacky for weeks. If you use raw oil, allow at least three days between coats to make sure that the oil has had plenty of time to dry. The drying times given in the directions below are for boiled linseed oil.

Open-Pore Oil Finish

It is often desirable to leave the pores of the wood open when you apply an oil finish. This leaves the wood with a natural-looking texture. This is the standard type of oil finish. It will protect the wood and will produce a gloss ranging from flat to medium, depending on the number of coats used. The directions given here are for a finish in which the pores are left open. If you want a smoother surface and a higher gloss, refer to the directions for a high-gloss oil finish in the next section.

The first coat of oil will rapidly soak into the wood. When this coat dries, it will partially seal the wood so that additional coats will not soak in as rapidly. If you are using a thin-bodied oil for the first coat, it can be applied straight. If the oil is thick-bodied, thin it with one part spirits of turpentine to 20 parts oil. If you are used to working with modern penetrating oils, you will have to change your procedure when using oils such as linseed oil.

Modern penetrating oils can be applied in a heavy, wet coat, because they are formulated to dry rapidly and harden even if a lot of oil has soaked into the wood. The usual procedure with these oils is to apply the oil with a brush or a rag in a heavy, wet coat; let it soak in for a few minutes, then wipe more oil on the dry spots; let the oil remain on the surface for about 15 minutes, adding more oil as necessary to keep the surface wet before wiping it off. If you use this technique with linseed oil or one of the other natural oils, the oil that has soaked into the wood will take a very long time to dry. The undried oil in the wood can bleed onto the surface at a later date, causing small spots of oil that will leave the surface glossier in some areas than the surrounding finish.

The best procedure for applying linseed oil is to apply it in very thin coats and allow each coat to dry overnight. Wipe the oil on with a rag and buff it using a lot of hand pressure (Illus. 8-2).

Illus. 8-2. The open-pore oil finish protects the wood while letting the natural texture of the pores show. It is a good choice for woods such as walnut or oak. Apply the oil with a soft rag and rub it in hard.

Wipe the oil off the surface before it starts to get gummy. Wipe it hard so that all of the oil left on the surface is removed. The only oil you want to remain is the oil that has soaked into the wood. Oil left on the surface will get tacky and attract dust.

Let the first coat of oil dry two days, to ensure that the oil has had a chance to polymerize. If you apply additional coats too soon, the first coat of oil may bleed through onto the surface, causing small spots that are glossier than the surrounding finish.

For the second coat of oil and all subsequent coats, use the undiluted oil. Wipe on a thin coat with a rag and buff it hard to generate some heat from the friction of the rag against the wood. The heat will force the oil into the wood and polish the finish. Make sure that you have wiped off all of the excess oil. Don't allow any wet oil to remain on the wood surface, or it can get gummy and attract dust.

You can apply as many additional coats of oil as you

feel is necessary to achieve the finish you want. Each additional coat of oil should be wiped on in a thin coat and then buffed off completely. Let each coat dry overnight, to give it a chance to absorb oxygen from the air before you apply another coat.

After the final coat has dried overnight, burnish the surface by rubbing it hard with a soft cloth. This will bring out the lustre of the finish. Using this procedure, you can get a soft satin gloss. It is even possible with many coats to get a medium gloss, but if you want a high gloss, you will have to use the procedure described in the next section.

High-Gloss Oil Finish

During the 18th century, a high-gloss finish was very fashionable. Linseed oil was often used to produce a high-gloss finish. The secret to producing a high gloss with an oil is to fill the pores of the wood and to use a specially prepared oil called "fat oil" for the final coats (Illus. 8-3).

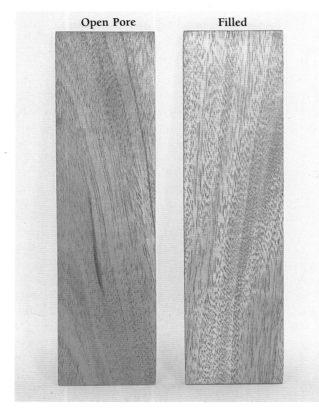

Open Pore **Filled**

Illus. 8-3. To produce a high gloss, you must fill the pores. The mahogany sample on the left has an open-pore finish. The sample on the right has had its pores filled with oil and pumice.

Apply the first coat following the general directions given above in the section Open-Pore Oil Finish. The second coat of oil should be applied with a filler when you are working with open-grained woods. Brick dust is a traditional filler used on red-colored mahogany. Thomas Sheraton recommends brick dust as a filler in his *Cabinet Dictionary,* published in 1803. See Illus. 8-4 for his directions on applying an oil finish.

THE

CABINET DICTIONARY

By T. SHERATON,

Author of the Cabinet-Maker and Upholsterer's Drawing Book.

The general mode of polishing plain cabinet work is however, with oil and brick-dust; in which case, the oil is either plain linseed or stained with alkanet root—SEE ALKANET ROOT. If the wood be hard, the oil should be left standing upon it for a week; but if soft, it may be polished in two days. The brick-dust and oil should then be rubbed together, which in a little time will become a putty under the rubbing cloth, in which state it should be kept under the cloth as much as possible; for this kind of putty will infallibly secure a fine polish by continued rubbing; and the polisher should by all means avoid the application of fresh brick-dust, by which the unskilful hand will frequently ruin his work instead of improving it: and to prevent the necessity of supplying himself with fresh brick-dust he ought to lay on a great quantity at first, carefully sifted through a gauze stocking; and he should notice if the oil be too dry on the surface of the work before he begin, for in this case it should be re-oiled, that it may compose a sufficient quantity of the polishing substance, which should never be altered after the polishing is commenced, and which ought to continue till the wood by repeated friction become warm, at which time it will finish in a bright polish, and is finally to be cleared off with the bran of wheaten flour.

Illus. 8-4. This excerpt from Thomas Sheraton's *Cabinet Dictionary* describes the process he recommends for applying an oil finish to mahogany.

Brick dust is made from red-clay bricks. Break up the brick with a hammer, and then grind the bits to dust with a mortar and pestle. Place the dust in a pounce bag and sprinkle the dust on the surface of the wood. The pounce bag will act as a filter, trapping any large pieces. Pumice is another traditional material; it makes a good filler for wood of any color.

The procedure given below works well on closed-grain woods and open-grained woods with small pores. It will take two or three applications of filler to completely fill the pores of mahogany, and it is also difficult to completely fill the pores of walnut; oak is almost impossible to fill completely.

Begin the filling procedure by wiping a coat of oil on the wood. You can use clear oil for this step, or you may want to use red oil for mahogany or tinted oil that matches the color of another type of wood. (See the formulas for red oil and tinted oil on page 82.) Using the colored oil will make the filler match the rest of the wood better.

Next, sprinkle brick dust or pumice onto the wet oil (Illus. 8-5). Apply more oil to a rag and rub the filler into the pores with a circular motion (Illus. 8-6). Keep rubbing the filler until all of the pumice has been wiped off the surface. Try not to wipe the filler out of the pores, but do remove all of the excess from other parts of the surface.

Finally, wipe the surface again with a clean rag to remove excess oil; then let the oil dry thoroughly. Since the filler absorbs a lot of oil, it is advisable to let the filler dry for three or more days before proceeding with the next coat. When the oil is dry, examine the surface. As the oil dries, the filler may shrink. If necessary, repeat the filling procedure.

After completing the filling step, you can build a gloss faster by using thickened oil. This thickened oil is often referred to as fat oil in old formulas. Stalker and Parker described fat oil in 1688 in their book *A Treatise of Japaning and Varnishing.*

Illus. 8-6. Use a rag to rub the pumice into the pores of the wood.

Fat oil is made by pouring the oil into a wide-mouth jar and exposing it to the air and sunlight for several weeks. Cover the top of the jar with a piece of cloth and tie it with a string. The cloth will let in air, but keep out dust. Gradually the oil will oxidize and the polymerization process will begin. This will thicken the oil. You won't notice much change in the oil for several weeks; then the oxidation process will speed up and there will be a thin skin on the surface of the oil. Stir the oil each day to mix the skin back into it. Continue doing this for another few weeks. When the oil is about the consistency of honey, it is ready to use (Illus. 8-7). Store the fat oil in a tightly capped container, to prevent further thickening.

To apply a coat of fat oil, use a soft cloth folded into a pad. Unfold the pad and pour some fat oil inside. Fat oil may contain small particles of oil that has hardened; this is called "seediness." When you pour the oil inside the cloth pad, the cloth will act as a strainer to trap the small particles.

Rub the oil onto the surface using a lot of hand pressure. Make the coat very thin. When you have applied a thin, even coat, let the oil dry overnight. If the surface is not tacky the next day, apply another coat of fat oil. If the surface is the least bit tacky, let it dry another day or until it feels completely dry. Keep applying coats of fat oil until you achieve a high gloss.

If the surface has picked up some dust, you can smooth it by rubbing it with pumice. Wipe some raw linseed oil on the surface and sprinkle on some pumice. Use a felt

Illus. 8-5. After applying a coat of oil, sprinkle pumice onto the wood surface. The pumice will mix with the wet oil to make a filler.

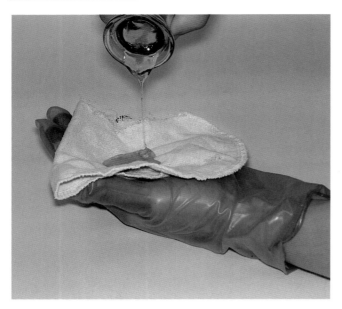

Illus. 8-7. Fat oil is linseed oil that has been thickened to the consistency of honey.

block to rub the surface until the dust nibs are gone. Wipe off the oil and pumice residue; then polish the surface with rottenstone or tripoli. Finally, give the work a coat of soft beeswax polish and buff it to a high gloss.

OIL-FINISH VARIATIONS

Oils may be mixed together with other oils or other ingredients to produce penetrating finishes that have better working properties, different colors, or more durability than the straight oil. The modern Danish oils and penetrating oil finishes that are sold commercially are these types of finish. Penetrating finishes made from several ingredients have been around for many years. The following sections describe how to make and use a few of them (Illus. 8-8).

Oil and Beeswax

A simple formula that has been used since at least the 1700's mixes 2 ounces of beeswax, one pint of spirits of turpentine, and one pint of linseed oil. Cut the beeswax into small pieces; a block plane shreds the beeswax well. Put the shredded wax into a glass container and pour on the spirits of turpentine. Seal the lid and let the container sit on a windowsill that receives sunlight for several days, shaking it occasionally until the beeswax is thoroughly dissolved. Now, pour in the linseed oil and mix the in-

gredients completely. To apply the finish, follow the general directions given above for the open-pore oil finish. You can apply several coats of oil first and then use the oil and beeswax for the final coat.

Red Oil

Red oil is linseed oil that has been tinted red with alkanet root. It has been traditionally used to enhance the color of mahogany. Thomas Sheraton recommended a red oil made with alkanet root, dragon's blood, and brazilwood, but most formulas simply use alkanet root.

To make red oil, bruise a few sticks of alkanet root by hitting them with a hammer or in a mortar with a pestle; then put them in a jar of spirits of turpentine or naphtha. Seal the jar and let the solvent absorb the color of the alkanet root for several weeks. Pour some of the colored solvent into another container, straining it through several layers of cloth.

Add the red solvent to linseed oil. The solvent will thin the oil. Usually, the thin consistency is desirable, because it lets the color soak deep into the wood. If the oil is too thin after adding the solvent, you can leave the lid off and cover the mouth of the jar with cloth as described in the section on fat oil, to thicken it.

Apply the red oil as the first and second coat of oil following the same procedure as described for a standard-oil finish.

Tinted Oil

Oil-soluble aniline dye can be used to tint oil to any color desired. The aniline dyes are more lightfast than the natural dyes, so by using a red mahogany aniline dye stain mixed with oil you can produce a red oil that will keep its color even after years of exposure to light. Brown-tinted oil is also useful when you are working with woods other than red mahogany. You can choose any of the colors available in oil-soluble dye stains.

The oil-soluble dyes come in a powder form. This powder is not completely soluble in oil; it must first be dissolved in a solvent; you can use spirits of turpentine or naphtha to dissolve the dye. Mix up a small amount of the dye and let it dissolve overnight. The next day, strain the dye through several layers of cloth to remove any undissolved particles; then add the dye to linseed oil a little at a time. Mix the dye into the oil and keep adding dye until you are satisfied with the color.

The tinted oil can be applied just like ordinary linseed oil. The oil will color the wood like a stain, but it penetrates deeply and it has a very transparent color, so it doesn't obscure the grain of the wood.

Linseed Oil   Walnut Oil   Oil and Beeswax   Red Oil   Brown Oil

Illus. 8-8. Shown here are the various types of oil finishes described in this chapter. The maple sample on the far left is finished with linseed oil. Notice that it is slightly darker than the sample next to it. The linseed oil will continue to darken with age. The next sample is maple finished with walnut oil. The walnut oil doesn't darken the natural color of the wood, and it won't darken with age; however, it is not as durable as linseed oil. The sample in the middle is walnut finished with linseed oil and beeswax. The beeswax gives the finish a soft lustre. The next sample to the right is mahogany finished with red oil. The red oil deepens the natural red color of the mahogany. The sample on the far right is cherry finished with brown oil. The brown oil acts like a transparent stain. It colors the wood without obscuring the grain.

CHAPTER NINE

Wax Finishes

WAX HAS PROBABLY been used as a wood-finishing material longer than any other product. Wax can be the complete finish or it can be used to protect and polish another type of finish. In the 1700's and 1800's, shellac and varnish were available, but wax was often used as the only top coat of a finish. When other top coats were used, a protective coat of wax was often added as the final coat.

Even during periods when varnish or shellac were the finish of choice by fine cabinetmakers, country craftsmen still used wax because it was readily available locally. In remote areas such as the American Southwest, beeswax was one of the few finishing products that was available. The Mission style of furniture that started around 1900 rejected the ornate and glossy look that had been popular and marked a return to simple finishes such as wax and oil. Even today, many woodworkers prefer the soft, natural look of a wax finish.

Wax makes a very good protective coating, because it is the most impervious to water of all of the natural finishing products. It is especially good at sealing wood against air humidity.

Wax is easy to apply, and it produces a beautiful finish, but it does have some disadvantages. Wax is relatively soft. This means that the protective film is easily damaged. Although the damage is easily repaired by adding another coat of wax, until more wax is applied the wood will be susceptible to water damage.

Another disadvantage of using a wax finish is that the method of applying wax to wood usually results in a very thin surface coating. Wax is very water-resistant, but a thin wax film is not sufficient to completely seal the wood from standing water. Water left on the surface will eventually soak through to the wood below; however, a thin film of wax will resist water long enough to allow you to wipe the surface dry.

A final disadvantage of using a wax finish is that dirt and dust can become embedded in the wax and get trapped in the pores of the wood. The dirt in the wax can also discolor the finish; however, this is part of the process that makes an antique look old, so a wax finish will age to a natural patina.

TYPES OF WAX

Beeswax has been used throughout history as a finishing wax (Illus. 9-1), but there are many other waxes that can be used. Prior to the 20th century, beeswax was used almost exclusively. If you find a reference to wax in an old recipe, it is beeswax.

Illus. 9-1. Beeswax has been used as a wood finish for centuries. Today, bees are raised in hives like this one. You can buy wax from beekeepers or wood-finishing companies. This one-pound block of beeswax is a convenient size for wood finishing.

Each wax has different qualities. Some waxes are harder than others and some will take a higher degree of polish; others are softer and easier to apply. By combining several waxes, a blend can be tailored for a specific purpose.

There are many commercially available wax blends. The sections below will provide some basic information about different waxes, so you can evaluate the ingredients found in commercially available wax blends to decide on the one that will best suit your purposes.

Beeswax

Beeswax is produced by the honey bee. The wax is made

from pollen gathered by the bees. The bees eat the pollen and then secrete the wax from special glands on their abdomens. The bees use the wax to build a honeycomb. The wax varies in color from light yellow to dark brown. The color depends on the type of pollen the bees have been eating. The palest-color wax is called "white wax," and the darkest wax is called "yellow wax." Yellow wax can be bleached to make it white.

The wax is harvested as a by-product of honey production. After the honey is extracted from the comb, the wax is washed in cold water and then melted in hot water. The liquid wax floats on top of the water, and is passed through strainers to remove contaminating material. Solar heat can be used to melt the wax. The sunlight also bleaches the wax to a lighter color. The wax can also be bleached by chemical processes.

Beeswax is completely insoluble in water. This makes it an ideal wood protectant. If the wax film is thick enough, it will completely seal the wood, but a thick film is usually aesthetically undesirable. When the wax is applied in a thin film, it will repel water and seal against atmospheric humidity, but it is not waterproof. The wax forms a flexible film that can be polished to a high gloss. It melts between 141 and 149 degrees Fahrenheit (61 and 65 degrees Celsius).

Beeswax is compatible with all other waxes; it can also be mixed with vegetable oils such as linseed oil. It will mix with mineral oil if the mixture is heated. Beeswax will dissolve in spirits of turpentine. It can also be dissolved in ethyl alcohol if heated.

Carnauba Wax

Carnauba wax is produced from a Brazilian palm tree (*Copernicia cerifera*). It was first exported from Brazil in about 1845. Two grades are available: The better grade is called Prime Yellow; the lower-quality grade is called Fatty Grey.

Carnauba wax is one of the hardest waxes; its melting point is between 183 and 196 degrees Fahrenheit (84 and 91 degrees Celsius). It can be polished to a high lustre. It is compatible with other waxes. When combined with beeswax, the melting point of the beeswax is raised and the resulting wax will be harder and can be polished to a high gloss.

Candelilla Wax

Candelilla wax is harvested from the stems of the *Pedilanthus pavinia* plant, which grows in Mexico. It is similar to carnauba wax in its properties, but it has a lower melting point of 152 to 158 degrees Fahrenheit (67 to 70 degrees Celsius). It began to be exported around 1913.

Paraffin

Paraffin is a petroleum product. It is obtained by distilling crude oil. The wax is white with a slightly bluish tint.

Paraffin wax is fairly soft. Its melting point is variable, depending on the oil and distillation process. Its melting temperature ranges from a low of 95 degrees Fahrenheit (35 degrees Celsius) to a high of 165 degrees Fahrenheit (75 degrees Celsius). The types with higher melting points are harder and can be polished to a high gloss. The main advantage of paraffin wax is its complete water resistance and its inert character, that is, that it does not chemically react with the wood or other finishing materials.

Microcrystalline

Microcrystalline is a special form of paraffin wax; it has an extremely fine crystal structure and greater hardness than ordinary paraffin wax. It is often used by museums for protecting the finish on valuable antiques, because it doesn't contain any ingredients that might react with the original finish and it can be completely removed if necessary without damaging the underlying finish.

Japan Wax

Japan wax comes from the berries of the sumac tree that grows in Japan, China, Southeast Asia, and India. This is the same tree that produces lacquer resin.

Japan wax is fairly soft and has a low melting point of 118 to 124 degrees Fahrenheit (48 to 53 degrees Celsius), but it does form a relatively tough and flexible film.

Ouricury

Ouricury is a wax produced by the palm tree *Syagrus coronata,* which grows in northern Brazil. It is very similar to carnauba wax in its properties except that it has a dark brown color.

Ouricury has a melting point of 163 to 185 degrees Fahrenheit (73–85 degrees Celsius). It is hard and lustrous, but slightly brittle. It can be polished to a high gloss. It can be used as a substitute for carnauba wax when a dark color is acceptable.

Ozokerite

Ozokerite is a mineral wax that can be quite hard, but its properties vary, depending on the deposits where it originates. When it is refined, it is sometimes called "ceresin."

Montan

Montan is a hard mineral wax. It is extracted from lignite or peat. It is similar to carnauba wax in most respects. Its melting point varies, depending on the deposits it was extracted from, but it is generally between 169 and 266 degrees Fahrenheit (76 and 130 degrees Celsius).

Lac Wax

Lac wax is secreted by the lac bug as it secretes lac resin. Lac wax is found in most shellac products unless they have been dewaxed. Lac wax is a by-product of the dewaxing process; when the shellac is filtered, the wax is separated from the shellac. The color of lac wax varies, depending on where the lac was gathered, ranging from light yellow to medium brown.

Lac wax is a hard wax that will improve the gloss of a wax blend. Its melting point is between 172 and 180 degrees Fahrenheit (78 and 82 degrees Celsius).

APPLYING A WAX FINISH

Wax has been used as the sole top coat on furniture for centuries. Thomas Sheraton gives a good explanation of the various ways wax was used in his 1803 book, the *Cabinet Dictionary*. (See Illus. 9-2.) Beeswax was the wax used, and it was applied either as hard wax (straight beeswax with no additives) or soft wax (a mixture of beeswax and balsam or spirits of turpentine). The hard wax produced a better shine, but it was more difficult to apply. The soft wax was easier to apply, but it didn't polish to as high a gloss. Beeswax was also mixed with linseed oil to make an oil-and-wax polish. (See Chapter Eight.)

A thin film of wax is colorless, but wax that builds up in the wood pores will look white or yellow. Sometimes dyes or pigments are added to the wax to color it to match the wood (Illus. 9-3).

Hard-Wax Polish

Using hard beeswax involves rubbing a lump of hard wax over the wood vigorously to generate enough heat to slightly melt the wax (Illus. 9-4). Working in the warm sun or near a heat source makes the process easier. Illustrations in old books show the polisher working near a heating stove.

Once the wax has been applied, it must be smoothed and polished. The hard wax is difficult to remove, so you can't simply wipe it off as you would a modern wax. Special techniques are necessary to remove the excess wax and force the wax deep into the pores of the wood. A cork block was sometimes used during the 19th century. It was rubbed hard over the wax, generating heat from friction as it was rubbed. This melts the wax and forces it into the pores of the wood (Illus. 9-5).

Another way to smooth the wax is to scrape it off with a dull scraper. Use an ordinary steel hand scraper, but remove the burr and dull the edge slightly by rounding it on a whetstone. The dull edge will scrape off the wax without damaging the wood (Illus. 9-6).

After the wax has been smoothed and forced into the pores, you can buff the wax to a gloss with a soft cloth.

Roubo's Hard-Wax Polish

This process of polishing wax to a high-gloss finish is described by Roubo in his 1769 book *The Art of the Woodworker*. The process begins before any wax is applied. The wood must be prepared and smoothed to a high degree.

THE

CABINET DICTIONARY

By T. SHERATON,

Author of the Cabinet-Maker and Upholsterer's Drawing Book.

POLISH—Is to give brightness to any substance. The method of polishing amongst cabinet-makers is various, as required in different pieces of work. Sometimes they polish with bees wax and a cork for inside work, where it would be improper to use oil. The cork is rubbed hard on the wax to spread it over the wood, and then they take fine brick-dust and sift it through a stocking on the wood, and with a cloth the dust is rubbed till it clears away all the clammings which the wax leaves on the surface.

At other times they polish with soft wax, which is a mixture of turpentine and bees wax, which renders it soft, and facilitates the work of polishing. Into this mixture a little red oil may occasionally be put, to help the colour of the wood. This kind of polishing requires no brick-dust; for the mixture being soft, a cloth of itself, will be sufficient to rub it off with.

Chairs are generally polished with a hardish composition of wax rubbed upon a polishing brush, with which the grain of the wood is impregnated with the composition, and afterward well rubbed off without any dust or bran. The composition I recommend is as follows: take bees wax and a small quantity of turpentine in a clean earthen pan, and set it over a fire till the wax unites with the turpentine, which it will do by constant stirring about; add to this a little red lead finely ground upon a stone, together with a small portion of fine Oxford ochre, to bring the whole to the colour of brisk mahogany. Lastly, when you take it off the fire, add a little copal varnish to it, and mix it well together, then turn the whole into a bason of water, and while it is yet warm, work it into a ball, with which the brush is to be rubbed as before observed. And observe, with a ball of wax and brush kept for this purpose entirely, furniture in general may be kept in good order.

Illus. 9-2. This excerpt from Thomas Sheraton's *Cabinet Dictionary* reveals several ways that wax was used as a wood finish in the 1700's and 1800's.

| Hard Wax | Soft Wax | Red Wax | Brown Wax | Black Wax |

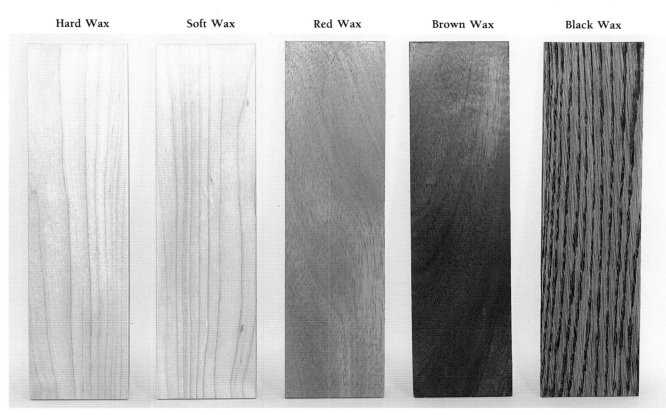

Illus. 9-3. These samples are finished with some of the types of beeswax discussed in this chapter. From left to right are hard wax, soft wax, red wax, brown wax, and black wax.

Illus. 9-4. The first step when applying a hard-wax finish is to rub the wood surface with a lump of beeswax.

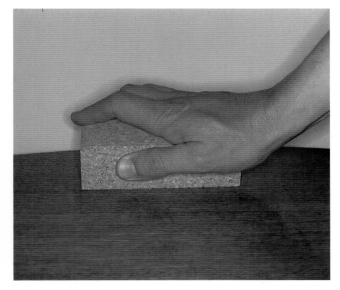

Illus. 9-5. Thomas Sheraton recommends polishing the hard wax with a cork block. Rub hard to melt the wax and smooth it.

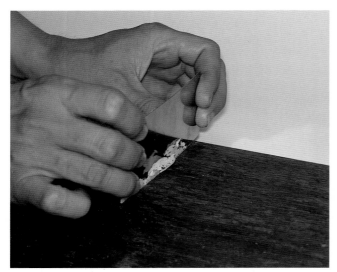

Illus. 9-6. Another way to smooth the wax is to scrape it level. Use a dull hand scraper.

If there are any imperfections in the wood, wax will only make them more visible.

Roubo suggests using scrapers, followed by sharkskin and finally scouring rush, to smooth the wood before waxing. The wax is applied with a rush polisher. This consists of a bundle of ordinary rush (marsh plants) tied up with string. You can gather rush in most areas near water.

Melt some wax in a double boiler. (A double boiler consists of two pans that fit together.) Dip the rush polisher into the melted wax. The porous stems of the rush will soak it up. Let the rush soak in the wax until it seems to have absorbed as much of the wax as possible; then remove it and let it cool.

To apply the wax, rub the end of the rush polisher vigorously over the wood. The rush stems burnish the wood as a thin coat of wax is applied (Illus. 9-7).

The rush polisher won't get into tight corners, mouldings, and carvings. Roubo recommends using a burnisher to apply the wax in these areas. These burnishers, or polishing sticks, are simply shop-made pieces of hardwood dowel with a pointed or flattened end. Various shapes and sizes of burnishers enable you to work into tight corners and mouldings. Rub the end of the burnisher against a block of hard wax, and then rub the wax onto the wood. Rub the burnisher hard over the surface of the wax until a high gloss is produced.

Soft-Wax Polish

Soft wax doesn't take as much effort to apply. The wax is applied as a soft paste. The wax will harden after the

Illus. 9-7. Roubo recommends a rush polisher for applying hard wax. The ends of the rushes burnish the wax to a high gloss.

solvents evaporate, and it can be buffed to a gloss. Soft wax can be used to produce a satin gloss, and it is useful when you want to maintain the texture of the wood instead of filling the pores completely with wax.

Commercially prepared soft beeswax is available from woodworking supply stores. It comes in a tin like other paste waxes. Modern paste waxes can be used as a substitute for soft beeswax. The techniques of application are the same. The modern paste waxes are a blend of several waxes and usually incorporate the harder waxes such as carnauba. They will be more durable than straight beeswax. The modern paste waxes are historically accurate for styles dating from about 1900 onwards. Mission furniture was often finished with these types of waxes.

Soft beeswax is simple to make. There are two types of soft wax: beeswax and balsam, and beeswax and spirits of turpentine. Information for making these two types of soft wax is given below.

● **Beeswax and Balsam** This traditional formula for soft wax is described by Thomas Sheraton in his *Cabinet Dictionary*. It uses balsam to soften the wax to the consistency of modern paste wax. Balsam is a liquid resin derived from coniferous trees such as pine, fir, spruce, balsam, and larch. It is usually called turpentine in old formulas. Don't confuse balsam with spirits of turpentine. Balsam contains resins and solvents. Spirits of turpentine are the distilled solvents from balsam.

Sheraton doesn't give exact proportions in his recipe, but I have found that about one ounce of balsam to one pound of beeswax works well. Of course, you don't have to make that much. You can make a smaller batch as long as you keep the proportions the same.

Begin by melting the beeswax in a double boiler. Put water in the bottom pan and the wax in the top pan. This will help to keep the wax from overheating. Wax can burn if heated too much, so be careful.

When the wax is completely liquidized, pour in the balsam. Stir the mixture thoroughly. Pour the wax into a container to cool. Choose a shallow, wide-mouthed container. An empty paste-wax tin is ideal.

When the wax has cooled, it is ready to use. Make a pad out of soft cloth and rub the cloth into the wax until the face of the pad is coated with wax. Now, rub the wax onto the wood using a circular motion.

Next, rub the wood with the grain, pressing down very hard to generate some heat from friction. This will melt the wax and force it into the wood. Let the wax harden for about 15 minutes; then buff the wax. After the wax has hardened for several days, buff it again to bring out the gloss.

• **Beeswax and Spirits of Turpentine** This is another traditional way to make soft wax: Beeswax and spirits of turpentine is softer than beeswax and balsam. It is about the same consistency as butter, and is the easiest type of beeswax to apply.

To start, cut some beeswax into small pieces. Old-time finishers used a plane to shave off slices of wax (Illus. 9-8). Put the wax in a glass or earthenware container and pour in an equal amount of spirits of turpentine. You can use naphtha instead of spirits of turpentine, if you want. Seal the container and let it sit in a warm area such as a sunny windowsill for several days, stirring it occasionally. When the wax is completely dissolved by the spirits of turpentine, it is ready to use (Illus. 9-9).

This soft wax can be applied to bare wood. Applying the wax to bare wood is the oldest method, but it is also traditional to apply a sealer coat of very thin shellac to the wood before applying the wax. Brush on a coat of one- or two-pound-cut shellac. The shellac will be completely absorbed by the wood and you won't see much of a surface film. Lightly sand the surface with fine sandpaper after the shellac is dry. The wax can be applied with a cloth or a brush. The cloth works better on closed-grained woods and the brush method is good for open-grained woods.

Illus. 9-8. To make soft wax, shave thin slices of wax off with a plane.

Illus. 9-9. When the wax is completely mixed with the spirits of turpentine, the soft wax is ready to use. It will be about the same consistency as soft butter.

To apply the wax with a cloth, dip a clean cloth into the wax, and then rub it over the wood surface in a circular motion. Rub it into the wood vigorously; then immediately use a second cloth to wipe off most of the excess wax.

Now, let the wax harden for about ten minutes; then, using a third cloth, buff the surface to the desired degree of polish. Just a little buffing will result in a satin gloss; more buffing can produce a higher gloss.

Let the wax harden for an hour or two and then repeat the process. You can keep adding coats of wax until you are satisfied with the finish.

If the wax is applied to bare wood, the first few coats will soak into the wood. After the wax has sealed the wood, a film will start to form and you will be able to polish it to a gloss. When the wax is applied over a sealer coat of shellac, the film will start to form on the first application of wax, but you should still apply several coats to get the maximum protection from the wax.

When you are applying wax to an open-grained wood and you want to preserve the natural texture of the wood and give it a satin sheen, you can use a brush to apply the wax and buff it. You will need two soft brushes. The best brushes are soft horsehair brushes used to shine shoes or brushes made for use on leather tack (saddles, etc.).

Dip the first brush into the wax and brush it over the wood using short, straight strokes with the grain. Work the wax into the pores by rocking the brush as you work. After the surface has been covered with wax, use the same brush to remove the excess. Don't add any more wax to the brush. Rub the brush over the surface in long, straight strokes with the grain. This will remove most of the wax from the pores and evenly distribute the wax on the surface.

Now, let the wax harden for about ten minutes; then go over the surface with the buffing brush. At first, work in short, rocking strokes to remove the remaining wax from the pores. Press down hard on the brush. Finish buffing by making long, straight strokes with the grain the full length of the wood. This will leave the wood with a soft satin gloss, and the texture of the grain will be visible.

Tinted Wax

When you apply wax to a dark, open-grained wood, the wax that builds up in the pores can turn white. This accentuates the pores and is usually not desirable. The traditional way to prevent this is to use a tinted wax. Tinted wax has a dye or pigment added to darken the color of the wax so that it will blend in with the color of the wood.

Tinted wax was probably used throughout the classic period of wood finishing (from the mid-1600's to the mid-1900's). Thomas Sheraton describes tinted wax in his *Cabinet Dictionary,* published in 1803, but it was probably in use long before that time. Tinted wax is available today in several shades of brown and black. It was frequently tinted red in earlier days.

Tinted wax doesn't stain the wood; it just colors the pores. If you to want to color the wood, you should apply a stain before you wax it (Illus. 9-10). You can use com-

mercially made tinted wax or make your own using the following formulas.

Illus. 9-10. Tinted wax colors the pores of the wood, but it doesn't add much color to the rest of the surface. If you want to darken the color of the wood, you must stain it first. The sample on the left is mahogany finished with only red wax. The sample on the right is mahogany stained first with dragon's blood stain and then finished with red wax.

• *Sheraton's Red Wax* This formula is based on a description of the waxing process found in Sheraton's *Cabinet Dictionary.* It is used on red mahogany or wood that has been stained red. Begin by making some red oil as described in Chapter Eight. Red oil is linseed oil that has been tinted red with alkanet root. Add one part red oil to ten parts soft wax and mix thoroughly.

The red wax can be applied using the directions given above for soft wax on page 88. If you want to fill the pores and give an open-grained wood a high gloss after applying the wax, sprinkle fine red-brick dust from a pounce bag over the surface. Work the brick dust into the pores using a rag. The dust will combine with the wax to produce a grain filler. Polish the surface with a clean rag.

The brick dust method can also be used to color hard wax. Hard wax is not tinted because doing so would turn it into soft wax. Instead, the wax is applied according to the directions given in the Hard-Wax Polish section on page 86. Then brick dust is applied to the surface and rubbed into the pores. This colors the wax in the pores. After wiping off the excess dust, polish the wax with a soft cloth.

• **Sheraton's Wax Balls** Thomas Sheraton describes wax balls that he says are used to polish chairs. In his *Cabinet Dictionary* he states that they are used by rubbing a brush over the wax ball and then brushing the wax onto the wood (Illus. 9-11). Use another brush to buff the wax. These wax balls can be used to finish any mahogany project; or, if you change the color of the pigments, they can be used for other types of wood.

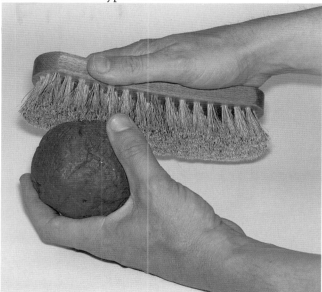

Illus. 9-11. Thomas Sheraton recommends rubbing a brush over wax balls and then brushing the wax onto the wood. This horsehair shoe-polishing brush works well. You can use this type of brush to apply any type of wax.

Here is the formula for Sheraton's wax balls:

¼ pound of beeswax

¼ ounce of balsam

Venetian red oil paint

Gold ochre oil paint

¼ ounce of oil-based copal varnish

Melt ¼ pound of beeswax in a double boiler; when it is liquefied, add ¼ ounce of balsam. Stir the balsam into the wax thoroughly, and then remove the mixture from the heat and add the rest of the ingredients.

Sheraton's formula used red lead and Oxford ochre as the colored pigments. Red lead is poisonous, so nowadays it should not be used. You can substitute another red pigment or any other color such as burnt umber or raw umber, depending on the color of finish you want. I use artist's oil paints to color the wax. They are linseed-oil-based, so they are compatible with the wax.

You can produce a good mahogany color by mixing a ½-inch-long squeeze from a tube of Venetian red (iron oxide) with a ½-inch-long squeeze from a tube of gold ochre. Mix the oil paints with ¼ ounce of artist's copal varnish. You can buy this type of oil-based copal varnish at an art-supply store. Pour the varnish and paint into the wax mixture and stir it all together. Pour the warm mixture into cool water and form it into a ball.

• **Black Wax** Black-tinted wax was often used on oak. The black wax accentuates the open-grain pattern of this wood and is very characteristic of old oak finishes. Black wax can be applied to the bare wood or over a shellac or varnish finish (Illus. 9-12).

Illus. 9-12. Black wax is a traditional way to accentuate the pattern of the pores on oak. When you apply the wax to bare wood or fumed oak, it will darken the color as shown by the sample in Illus. 9-3. This photo shows oak that has been varnished first and then polished with black wax. Applying varnish or shellac first increases the contrast between the black pores and the rest of the wood.

To make black wax, add some lampblack to soft wax. You can also use black artist's oil paint. Apply the wax using the methods described in the section Soft-Wax Polish on page 88. Wipe the wax on with a rag or brush and work it into the pores; then buff it with a rag or brush. The objective is to have the wax accumulate in the pores to accentuate them, so if you use a brush, don't brush so hard that you remove most of the wax from the pores. Black wax left on the surface of the wood can rub off on clothing, so keep buffing the wax until you can wipe a white cloth over the surface without picking up any black wax.

• **Brown Wax** Brown wax is useful when you want to make the wax in the pores of the wood blend with a dark brown wood (Illus. 9-13). Several shades of brown wax are sold today. You can get brown paste wax that is a blend of hard waxes, or you can get tinted beeswax.

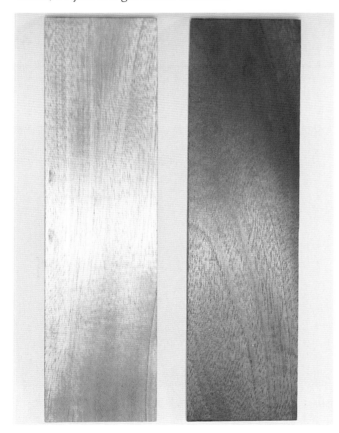

Illus. 9-13. Brown wax works well on any dark brown wood. These samples show brown wax on bare mahogany (left), and brown wax on mahogany that was first stained with walnut-husk stain. See Chapter Ten for details about stains.

You can also make your own brown wax by adding artist's oil paint to soft wax. Use raw umber for a light yellowish brown, or burnt umber for a dark brown. You can also mix other paint color to get any color of wax that you want. Just a small amount of oil paint will tint a large amount of wax, so add the paint in very small amounts. Another way to make brown wax is to add some brown-tinted linseed oil to soft wax. (See Chapter Eight for details about brown oil.) Apply brown wax as you would black wax.

WAX POLISHING ON THE LATHE

Wax is a good finish to apply to turnings while they are still on the lathe. Applying the wax to a rotating turning will generate enough friction to melt the wax, and the wood can be polished to a high gloss. Before applying the wax, make the turning as smooth as you can.

You can use very fine sandpaper to smooth the wood as the lathe rotates. A traditional way to smooth lathe turnings is to take a handful of wood shavings and press them against the rotating work.

The simplest type of wax finish is the hard-wax finish. To apply a hard-wax finish, just hold a lump of hard wax against the work as it rotates on the lathe (Illus. 9-14). The wax will soften and rub off onto the wood.

When the wood is completely covered with wax, buff the wax by holding a rag against the rotating work. Press the rag hard against the work. Hold the rag in one spot

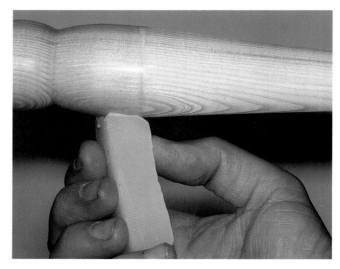

Illus. 9-14. Hard beeswax makes a good finish for lathe turnings. Hold a lump of wax against the rotating work. After the wood is covered with wax, buff it with a soft cloth held against the rotating work.

long enough to melt the wax, and then slowly move the rag from one end of the turning to the other.

You can also apply soft wax to a turning on the lathe. You can use the soft beeswax formulas described above or a commercial paste wax. Dip a rag into the wax; then apply it to the wood as it spins on the lathe. Let it harden for a few minutes, and then buff it with a soft cloth as the lathe spins. Several coats will be necessary to build up a good film of wax.

I have found that Sheraton's wax balls also make a very good lathe finish. They are easier to use if you form the wax into the shape of a stick instead of a ball. They don't have to be red; you can use any color of pigment you want. Burnt umber artist's oil paint makes a dark brown wax. You can also use an oil-soluble aniline dye dissolved in a small amount of linseed oil.

Press the wax against the wood as the lathe rotates, applying the wax to the entire surface (Illus. 9-15). Next, use a soft cloth to buff the wax. Press the cloth against the rotating work. Keep buffing until the desired gloss is produced. You can apply repeated applications until you achieve the desired finish.

USING WAX TO PROTECT OTHER FINISHES

Wax can be used to protect any other type of finish. It can be applied over shellac, oil, varnish, and all of the modern finishes (Illus. 9-16). Wax will restore the gloss to a surface that has become dull from wear. This is achieved when the surface is made as smooth and free

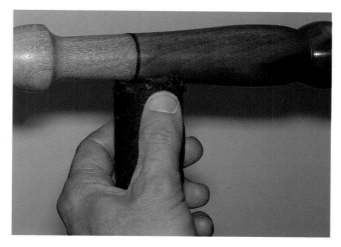

Illus. 9-15. You can use the formula given in this chapter for Sheraton's wax balls to make lathe finishing sticks.

from scratches as possible. Dust is a fine abrasive; normal use of furniture rubs dust across the surface, leaving microscopic scratches in the finish. These scratches dull the gloss. Wax restores the gloss by filling in the scratches.

Wax also leaves a thin film on the surface. When a wax film is present, the wear that would otherwise scratch the finish scratches the wax film instead. The wax is a sacrificial protectant. It is damaged by the wear, but, since wax is easily restored by another application, regular waxing will protect the underlying finish from wear.

Illus. 9-16. Wax will protect and beautify any type of wood finish. Apply the wax with a soft cloth or a brush. Buff the wax with a clean cloth.

Paste wax is the traditional choice for furniture polishing. The beeswax-and-balsam finish described on pages 88 and 89 can be used as a paste wax to protect other finishes. Thomas Sheraton recommends the wax balls described earlier as a good wax for maintaining the beauty of a finish. Modern paste wax is made of a blend of waxes softened with a small amount of solvent.

Paste wax is applied with a soft cloth or a waxing brush. Apply the wax in a circular motion. After wiping on the wax, use another cloth or brush to wipe off most of the wax left on the surface; then let the wax harden for about ten minutes and buff it to a gloss with a third clean cloth.

As you rub on the wax, it is forced into the small scratches in the surface. Wiping off the excess wax levels the surface, leaving the scratches full of wax and removing most of the excess on the surrounding finish.

As the solvent evaporates, the wax will harden. When it is hard, it can be buffed without removing it from the scratches. Buffing levels the surface and leaves a thin film of wax. The film is thicker where there are scratches and thinner where the surface of the finish is undamaged, resulting in a smooth, level top surface that will reflect light evenly, creating a high gloss.

CHAPTER TEN

Stains

STAINS ARE USED to change the color of wood or to emphasize its natural color. Stains were used during the 1600's and 1700's, but probably not as frequently as they are today. Stains were widely used during the 1800's.

There are two basic types of stains: dye stains and pigment stains. Almost all of the stains used during the classic period of wood finishing were dye stains. Dye stains are transparent, and they soak deep into the wood. This enhances the natural beauty of the wood, and the color of the finish seems to originate from inside the wood. Dye stains are usually water- or alcohol-soluble.

Pigment stains became more common after about 1940. They are the type most often sold today. A pigment stain contains finely ground minerals suspended in a varnish-like vehicle. The result is really a very thin paint. When it is wiped on the wood, the pigments fill the pores and get trapped in the tiny scratches on the surface of the wood. Pigment stains are easy to apply, and they are very lightfast, but they usually look a little muddy (lacking in brightness), and they obscure the grain slightly.

In this book, I will only discuss the dye stains. If you want more information on pigment stains, consult my other books, *Wood Finisher's Handbook* and *Finishing Basics*. Dye stains can be subdivided into stains that are made from natural dyestuffs and synthetic dye stains.

Many dye stains are water-based. When water is applied to wood, it causes small fibres to stand up on the surface of the wood. After the wood dries, some of these fibres remain standing, giving the wood a rough texture. This is called "raised grain." Chapter Two describes how to prepare the wood so that raised grain won't be a problem; however, there will always be a few raised fibres. After the stain dries, you will usually have to lightly sand it with very fine sandpaper, being careful not to sand through the stain.

Dye stains can be applied with a damp sponge, a rag, or a brush. A bristle brush cannot be used, because water will soften the bristles. The traditional type of brush was made from plant fibres that won't go limp when wet, for example, tampico, a fibre that comes from cactus. Tampico won't go limp when wet, and it is resistant to chemicals,

Illus. 10-1. Classic stains are more difficult to apply than the modern wiping stains. To get an even color, apply several coats of diluted stain instead of one coat of strong stain. You can apply the stains with a rag, a sponge, or a brush. Here, I am using a rag to apply dragon's-blood stain to a cherry tabletop.

so it was often used as a staining brush. You can use one of the synthetic brushes such as a nylon or polyester brush for applying water stains, or you can use a foam brush.

If you are familiar with using modern pigmented wiping stains, you will have to completely change your staining technique. A wiping stain can be applied slowly, and any lap marks or unevenness can be corrected when wiping off the stain with a rag. When you apply dye stains, however, take care to apply them evenly. Dye stains soak into the wood quickly, and lap marks or uneven application will show up in the final finish if you are not careful when applying the stains. Work quickly and don't let the stain from one stroke dry before you apply the next stroke; if you do, dark lap marks may occur. You will get a more even color if you use diluted stain and apply several coats (Illus. 10-1). This enables you to slowly build up the color to the desired intensity. You can even-out color variations in the wood by applying additional coats to the light areas.

Veneers used for marquetry are often dyed. Many pieces of veneer can be soaked in a large tub of dye until the dye completely penetrates the wood. Individual pieces of veneer can be dyed by applying the dye to the back of the piece and keeping it wet with dye until the dye soaks through to the front. Veneers dyed in this manner can be scraped and sanded without fear of cutting through the dye.

NATURAL DYE STAINS

Natural dye stains are derived from plants or insects. The same dyes were used for many different crafts; these dyes were used by dyers to color cloth, by painters to make paint, and by wood finishers to stain wood.

Natural dyes produce beautiful, clear colors, but most have a major shortcoming: They are not lightfast. This means that after prolonged exposure to sunlight the colors fade or change color. Some of the original colors may not have survived more than ten years. This was well known at the time, and homemakers made every effort to preserve the color of their furniture by pulling window drapes when a room was not in use and even covering the furniture with throw cloths. Books containing advice to homemakers of the time suggested that furniture should be kept out of direct sunlight.

The colors that we see today on antique furniture are the results of the sun fading and aging the wood and finishing materials. Most people would be surprised to see the original colors. During the 1700's, wood was often stained bright-red. Yellow and black stains were also popular. After many years, the stains faded and the varnishes

darkened, giving the wood and the dark-amber color we associate with antique furniture. You can sometimes still see traces of the original color by removing the brass hardware. Brass hardware protects the wood below it from

Illus. 10-2. Most of the natural stains fade when exposed to sunlight. You can get a better idea of what an old finish originally looked like by removing one of the brass pulls on the piece of furniture.

direct sunlight, and some of the original color is preserved (Illus. 10-2).

If you want total accuracy in a period finish, you can use natural dye stains and accept the fact that they will eventually fade. This can be used to advantage when you want the piece to look just like a particular antique by deliberately exposing it to direct sunlight for an extended time. Eventually, the finish will fade to the same colors found on the original today.

If you want to duplicate the original color of the period, but you want a more permanent finish, you can still use natural dyes to an advantage. Mix up a small quantity of the stain and apply it to a piece of the same wood that you will be using in the project. This will give you a color sample that shows how that stain will appear on that particular type of wood. Use the natural-dye sample as a guide to make up a synthetic water stain, then stain the project with the synthetic dye stain.

Most natural stains come from plants, although some are derived from insects. Some of them are still sold in their natural state. Roots, seeds, and pieces of wood are all used to make dyes (Illus. 10-3). Many natural stains are sold as extracts. Extracts have been made for centuries. To make an extract, the plant material is processed to remove the dye; then the dye extract is concentrated and

Illus. 10-3. Most natural stains are derived from plant materials such as roots and seeds. Shown here are alkanet root (left), seeds from the annatto tree (middle), and madder root (right).

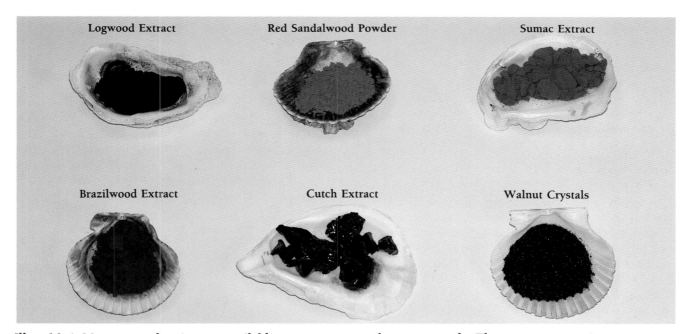

Illus. 10-4. Many natural stains are available as extracts, powders, or crystals. These types are easier to use because they are concentrated and dissolve easily. Shown on the top row from left to right are logwood extract, red sandalwood powder, and sumac extract. Shown on the bottom right from left to right are brazilwood extract, cutch extract, and walnut crystals.

dried to make a powder or crystals (Illus. 10-4). The extracts are easier to use because they are concentrated and dissolve easily.

In the sections that follow, I describe most of the natural dyestuffs that were used to make stains for wood. Many of these are still available today from specialty wood-finishing companies.

Alkanet Root

Alkanet root comes from the *Alkanna tinctoria* and related

plants. It produces a deep red dye. Alkanet dye is oil-soluble, making it very useful for tinting linseed oil, other oils, and varnishes. To extract the dye, bruise the root by hitting it with a hammer or in a mortar with a pestle; then soak the root in oil, spirits of turpentine, or naphtha.

Annatto Seeds

Annatto seeds come from the *Bixa orellana* tree. They were mostly used as a food coloring, but they can be used to make a reddish yellow or brown wood stain. Crush the seeds in a mortar with a pestle and boil them in water to make a water stain, or soak them in alcohol to make a spirit stain. Strain the liquid.

Brazilwood

Brazilwood produces a red dye. Brazilwood comes from several related trees in the *Caesalpincia* species. Brazilwood has been used as a red dye in Europe since the 1100's. The wood was imported from Ceylon and India. The South American country of Brazil received its name because large forests of brazilwood were found there. The dye is usually available today as brazilwood extract. The extract dissolves in warm water.

Buckthorn

The berries of the buckthorn shrub (*Rhamnus cathartica*) produce a yellow dye. Buckthorn dye was being used in Italy by the 1400's and in France by the 1600's. The berries are sometimes referred to as Persian Berries or Grains of Avignon in old formulas. To extract the dye, crush the berries and boil them in water.

Cutch

Cutch, also called catechu, is extracted from the trunk of the catechu tree, which grows in India, or from the leaves of the creeping catechu plant of Indonesia and Ceylon. It will produce a variety of browns ranging from chocolate-brown to light beige, depending on the mordant used. (See pages 99–102 for a discussion of mordants.) It is usually sold as an extract that will dissolve in warm water or alcohol.

Dragon's Blood

Dragon's blood is a resin produced by the rattan palm (*Calamus draco*), which grows in eastern Asia. It is blood-red in color. One of the main advantages of dragon's blood is that it will dissolve in alcohol, so it can be used to make spirit stain or to tint spirit varnishes.

Fustic

Fustic is a yellowwood from the *Chlorophora tinctoria* family. It produces a yellow dye. It is available as an extract that dissolves in warm water.

Gamboge

Gamboge is a yellow resin produced by trees in the *Garcinia* genus, which grow in India. It was imported to Europe probably as early as the Middle Ages. Since it is a resin and is alcohol-soluble, it was often used to tint spirit varnishes yellow. It can also be used to make a yellow spirit stain.

Henna

Henna is a reddish brown dye obtained from the henna plant (*Lawsonia inermis*). It was mostly used as a natural hair dye, but it can be used to dye wood. It comes as a powder that will dissolve in hot water.

Indigo

Indigo was one of the most important textile dyes. It is produced by the indigo plant (*Indigofera tinctoria*) and makes a rich blue dye. It was rarely used by woodworkers, because there was not much call for blue woodwork, but it was sometimes used to dye veneers used for marquetry. However, indigo does play an important role in the development of wood stains, because it was scientific research on indigo that led to the discovery of aniline dyes.

Logwood

Logwood is also called compeachy wood. It is the wood of the *Haematoxylon campechianum* tree. The wood itself or a powdered extract can be used to make stains. It can be used to produce a variety of colors, depending on the mordant used, that range from yellow to olive to brown. The extract will dissolve in warm water.

Madder

Madder The root of the madder plant (*Rubia tinctorum*) produces a red dye. Madder root dye was used as early as ancient Egyptian times. Madder became an important dye-stuff in Europe in the 1700's. When madder is combined with alum, it produces an orange-red color that is very brilliant and transparent.

The chemical that produces the color in madder root is called alizarin. This chemical was identified and made synthetically in the mid-1800's. The synthetic alizarin behaves like madder root and can be substituted in formulas that specify the use of madder root.

To extract the dye from madder root, break the roots into small pieces and boil them in water.

Sandalwood

Sandalwood is wood from the sandalwood tree; it can be

red or yellow. Red or yellow dye can be extracted from sandalwood. The dye is alcohol-soluble, so it is useful for making spirit stain or for tinting spirit varnish. Sandalwood is available as a powder. To extract the dye, put the powder in a jar with alcohol. Let the dye dissolve for several days; then strain the liquid.

Sandalwood is also partially soluble in water. Boil the powder in water and strain it.

Sumac Extract

Sumac Extract is an extract from the sumac plant. It is high in tannin. It will produce a variety of brown colors when treated with various mordants. (See the section on mordants on pages 99–102.) The extract will dissolve in warm water.

Weld

The leaves and seeds of the weld plant (*Reseda luteola*) produce a yellow dye. Weld is also called "dyer's herb" or "dyer's rocket." In the 1400's, weld was used to make a pigment called arzica. Arzica is the most lightfast of the natural yellow pigments. The weld plant still grows wild around the Mediterranean Sea, but it is no longer harvested as a dyestuff.

Weld is soluble in alcohol, so it can be used to make spirit stain. It can also be dissolved in hot water. It was probably most often used as tinting varnish for lutes and violins.

Walnut Husks

The fleshy outside husks of black walnuts produce a deep brown stain. The husks start out green and gradually turn dark brown. Let the husks turn brown before using them to make stain. Walnut husks are one of the easiest of the natural dyestuffs to obtain.

Yellowwood

Yellowwood is a tree in the *Cladrastis lutea* family. The dye is alcohol-soluble, so it can be used to make a yellow spirit stain or to tint spirit varnish.

Cochineal

Cochineal is a red dye made from the bodies of the cochineal insect (family *Coccus cacti*). Cochineal dye was used in Mexico and Guatemala long before Europeans arrived. After the Spanish explored Mexico in 1518, shipments of cochineal soon began to arrive in Europe. By 1549, it was an important dyestuff in Europe.

Kermes

Kermes is a red dye made from the dried bodies of a small insect from the family *Kermes ilicis* that lives in Southern France and Spain. Kermes was used as early as ancient Egyptian times as a dye. It was an important dye in Europe until the introduction of lac dye.

Lac

The same lac bugs that produce shellac make a red dye. The stick-lac is collected from trees where the bugs have laid their eggs. The lac is colored with a red-orange dye. The first stage in processing lac is to wash out as much of this dye as possible. The remaining dye is what gives orange shellac its color.

Lac dye was at one time more valuable than the lac resin. It was introduced to Europe by the Arabs in the 7th century AD. The color of the lac dye depends on the region where it was harvested. Kusumi lac is pale yellow, Siam lac is dark red, and Assam lac is pale red. Lac from south of Calcutta is red, and lac from north of the city is yellow or orange.

Walnut Crystals

Walnut Crystals produce a rich-brown walnut color. They are made from ancient peat beds found in the region around the city of Kassel in Germany. The crystals dissolve in warm water. In old formulas, they may be called Vandyke crystals or kassel extract.

Making Natural Water Stains

Most of the natural stains are water stains, that is, the dye is soluble in water. To prepare the stains, first dissolve the dye in water. If you are using an extract, you can usually dissolve it in warm water. Let the extract dissolve overnight. If you are using the raw plant materials such as leaves, roots, berries, or wood chips, then crush the plant material as much as possible in a mortar and pestle and boil it in water for one hour or longer. Start with a lot of water and let it boil until it almost evaporates, to concentrate the dye.

Before you apply the stain, strain the liquid through several layers of cloth or a piece of filter paper (a coffee filter will work).

• *Mordants* Most natural water-stain formulas specify the use of mordants. A mordant is a chemical applied to the wood to either change the color of the stain or to fix the stain, making it more permanent (Illus. 10-5). The name derives from the Latin word *mordere,* which means "to bite." A mordant makes the stain "bite" onto the wood.

Chemical mordants can be hazardous; be sure to wear protective gloves, goggles, and clothing when using them.

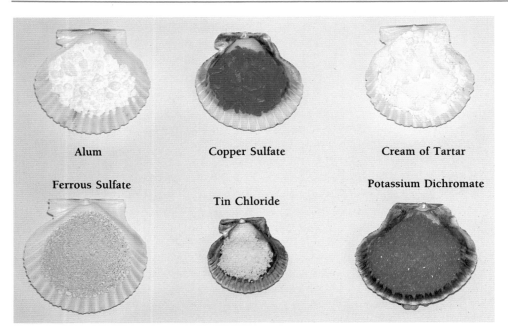

Illus. 10-5. Mordants are chemicals that change the color of a dye and make it more permanent. The mordants shown on the top row, from left to right, are alum (potassium aluminum sulfate), copper sulfate, and cream of tartar. The mordants shown on the bottom row, from left to right, are ferrous sulfate, tin chloride, and potassium dichromate.

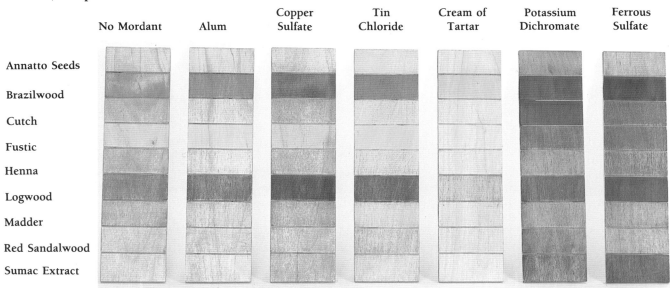

Illus. 10-6. Each mordant will alter the color of a natural dye in a slightly different way. These maple samples illustrate the effects of various mordants on a variety of natural stains. The stains in all seven columns of samples, from top to bottom, are annatto seed, brazilwood, cutch, fustic, henna, logwood, madder, red sandalwood, and sumac extract. The mordants that are used exclusively in each of the seven rows, from far left to right, are no mordant, potassium aluminum sulfate, copper sulfate, tin chloride, cream of tartar, potassium dichromate, and ferrous sulfate.

Be particularly careful when using acids. (See Chapter Eleven for more safety precautions concerning the use of chemicals.)

Mordants are usually applied separately to the wood, in some cases before the stain is applied and in other cases after the stain is applied. This results in a chemical change inside the wood that locks the dye in place. In a few formulas, the chemicals are added to the stain before application, but this is the exception, not the rule. Here is a list of some common mordants: *alum* (potassium aluminum sulfate), *ammonia, copper sulfate, cream of tartar, ferrous sulfate* (copperas), *Glauber's salt, muriatic acid, nitric acid* (aquafortis), *potassium dichromate, pyrogallic acid, sulfuric acid* (oil of vitriol), *tannic acid, tin chloride* (stannous chloride), and *vinegar* (acetic acid). Chapter Eleven gives more information on these chemicals; in this chapter, I only describe how they are used as mordants in the stain formulas below.

Each mordant will have a different effect on the various natural water stains. Illus. 10-6 shows some test samples that reveal the effects of some mordants on different natural dyes.

• *Natural Water-Stain Formulas* The following are based on traditional formulas used during the 1700's and early 1800's. Illus. 10-7 shows samples that have been stained using these formulas. After staining, the samples were given an oil finish to accentuate the color and show how it appears when the finish is complete.

Walnut Husk Stain This is one of the easiest natural stains to make and use, the ingredients are easy to find, and it produces a beautiful brown-walnut color. The French call this stain *brou de noix* (brew of walnut):

   1 quart of household-strength ammonia

   1 cup of walnut husks

Place the walnut husks in the ammonia and let the mixture sit for several days. The longer the husks remain in the ammonia, the stronger the stain will be; you can add more husks if you want a stronger stain. Pour off the liquid through a strainer. You can lighten the color by diluting the stain with water. Brush the stain on evenly and let it dry.

Walnut Crystal Stain Walnut crystals produce a deep walnut color that is very natural-looking. The intensity of the stain can be varied by using more or less water. Here is the formula:

   1 ounce of walnut crystals
   1 quart of water
   ½ cup of household-strength ammonia

Walnut Husk Stain	Walnut Crystal Stain	Brazilwood and Alum	Brazilwood and Tin Chloride	Black Logwood

Illus. 10-7. These samples have been stained using the natural water stain formulas in this chapter. They are, from left to right, walnut husk stain on mahogany, walnut crystal stain on maple, brazilwood and alum on mahogany, brazilwood and tin chloride on cherry, and black logwood on maple.

Bring the water to a boil and remove the water from the heat source. Add the crystals and stir. Let the crystals dissolve overnight and then pour the stain through a strainer to remove any undissolved sediment. Add about ½ cup of household ammonia. The ammonia deepens the color and makes it more permanent.

Mahogany Red Stain In the 1700's, red mahogany was very fashionable. Brazilwood stain was sometimes used to enhance the color of mahogany or to dye other types of wood red.

STAIN:

   1 ounce of brazilwood extract

   1 quart of water

MORDANT:

   1 ounce of alum (potassium aluminum sulfate)

   1 quart of water

Heat the water, and then add the brazilwood extract. Let the extract dissolve overnight, and then strain the liquid. To prepare the mordant, add the alum to room-temperature water. Let the alum dissolve overnight.

Apply the stain to the wood. For an intense color, apply several coats. After applying the last coat of stain, brush on the mordant. You will see an immediate change in the color.

Bright Red Stain You can make a very bright red stain using brazilwood and tin chloride.

STAIN:

   1 ounce of brazilwood extract

   1 quart of water

MORDANT:

   1 ounce of tin chloride

   1 quart of water

Dissolve the brazilwood extract in hot water and let it sit overnight: then strain the liquid through cloth or filter paper. Prepare the mordant by adding the tin chloride to room-temperature water. Let the tin chloride dissolve overnight.

Apply two or three coats of the stain to the wood with a brush, rag, or damp sponge. After applying the last coat of stain, apply the mordant.

Black Stain Black stains were often used to imitate the black lacquer found on Oriental furniture that was very popular in the 1700's.

STAIN:

   1 ounce of logwood extract

   1 quart of water

MORDANT:

   1 ounce of ferrous sulfate

   1 quart of water

Dissolve the logwood extract in hot water and let it sit overnight; then strain the liquid. Prepare the mordant by adding the ferrous sulfate to room-temperature water.

Apply two or three coats of the stain to the wood until the wood is a deep brown. After the last coat of stain, apply the mordant. The ferrous sulfate will turn the logwood stain black. You can apply several coats of the mordant to deepen the black. If it is not black enough, you can add more coats of logwood stain, followed by more ferrous sulfate. While the wood is wet, it will look black. When it dries, it will look grey, but when you apply oil, wax, shellac, or varnish, the deep black color will return.

Making Natural Spirit Stains

Spirit stains use alcohol as the solvent instead of water. Spirit stains won't raise the grain. Spirit stains dry quickly, so you can apply a top coat the same day.

Because the stain dries so quickly, it is more difficult

Illus. 10-8. Gamboge resin (left) and dragon's-blood resin (right) are the two most common ingredients in natural spirit stains.

Illus. 10-9. Spirit stains won't raise the grain of the wood. These samples show four types of spirit stain. From left to right, they are dragon's-blood stain on mahogany, red sandalwood stain on mahogany, gamboge stain on pine, and annatto stain on oak.

to apply. Lap marks can be a problem. To help avoid these, dilute the stain with alcohol and apply several coats until you get the desired color intensity.

The two most widely used spirit-stain ingredients are dragon's blood and gamboge (Illus. 10-8). Dragon's blood is the resin from the rattan palm. It produces a blood-red color. In ancient times, many people believed that it was actually the dried blood of a dragon. Gamboge is a yellow resin from trees in the *Garcinia* genus. It produces a yellow stain. Other alcohol-soluble dyes can also be used to make spirit stains; they include sandalwood, weld, cutch, annatto seeds, and yellowwood.

Illus. 10-9 shows samples that have been stained using the formulas below. I have given the samples an oil finish to accentuate the color as it will appear when a top coat is applied.

• **Spirit-Stain Formulas** Dragon's blood stain was probably the most widely used spirit stain in the 1600's and 1700's, but other spirit stains were occasionally used. Illus. 10-7 shows samples stained using the formulas below.

Dragon's Blood Stain This is a blood-red stain that will deepen the color of mahogany or stain other types of wood to imitate red mahogany. Here is the formula:

2 ounces of dragon's blood

1 quart of ethyl alcohol (shellac thinner)

Break the dragon's blood into small pieces with a mortar and pestle. Place the dragon's blood in the alcohol and shake it. Put the bottle in a sunlit area and shake it occasionally until the dragon's blood is dissolved. Strain the liquid to remove foreign material that was embedded in the resin.

Red Sandalwood Stain This is a brighter red than dragon's blood stain. Here is the formula:

2 ounces of red sandalwood powder

1 quart of ethyl alcohol (shellac thinner)

Mix the alcohol and the powder together and let the mixture sit in a warm place for several days. Strain the liquid to remove the wood fibres.

Gamboge Stain This stain will produce a bright yellow color on light woods; it will also enhance the color of darker woods. It gives oak a golden color. Here is the formula:

2 ounces of gamboge resin

1 quart of ethyl alcohol (shellac thinner)

Mix the alcohol and the gamboge resin and let the mixture dissolve for several days; then strain the liquid.

Annatto Stain This stain will produce a bright orange color on light woods; it will also enhance the color of darker woods. Here is the formula:

2 ounces of annatto seeds

1 quart of ethyl alcohol (shellac thinner)

Crush the seeds and let them soak in the alcohol for several days; then strain the liquid.

SYNTHETIC DYE STAINS

In the mid-19th century, the work of several scientists resulted in the development of synthetic dyes that were cheaper and more lightfast than the natural dyes. Soon after their development, these synthetic dyes became the main ingredients in most wood stains of the later 1800's and continued to be the dominant wood-finishing stains up until about 1940, when oil-based pigmented stains became popular. But even today, aniline stains are the basis of most industrial stains and some commercial products. Aniline stains are still sold in dry form for the advanced amateur and professional wood finisher (Illus. 10-10).

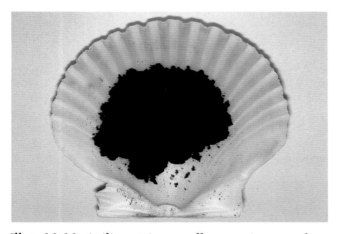

Illus. 10-10. Aniline stains usually come in a powder form. The powdered stain shown here is the walnut spirit stain used to stain the middle sample in Illus. 10-11.

In 1826, two French scientists named Robiquet and Colin isolated the main colorant in madder. This colorant is a chemical called alizarin.

Experiments with indigo dye resulted in the identification of one of the chemicals found in indigo. This chemical was given the name "aniline," based on the Indian name of the indigo plant—*anil*.

In the 19th century, gas illumination was introduced on a large scale. Many coal gasification plants were built to provide illuminating gas. A by-product of coal gasification was coal tar. At first, coal tar was considered a useless waste product of the process, but attempts were made to find uses for this substance that was being produced in such large quantities. After scientific study of coal tar, it was found that many useful products could be made from it. One of these products was synthetic aniline.

In 1856, William Henry Perkin, a British chemist, was experimenting with aniline in an attempt to make synthetic quinine (a drug used to treat malaria). He failed to make quinine, but he did discover a reddish purple dye. He called this dye "mauve." Mauve was a big success as a textile dye, but of little use to wood finishers; however, the development of this first aniline dye opened the door to a whole new industry.

In 1868, Perkin made synthetic alizarin through a chemical process. Two German scientists, Graebe and Lieberman, working independently of Perkin, also synthesized alizarin. The Germans were the first to patent the process, creating the basis of a new German dye industry. The synthetic alizarin was cheaper to produce than natural madder root, so it quickly dominated the market for red dye.

Within a few years, factories in Britain and Germany were making many different colors of synthetic dyes. Because the first of this class of synthetic dyes were made from aniline, the name aniline dye is usually applied to all of these synthetic dyes, even though many are now made with other chemicals. In old formulas, aniline dyes are often called "coal-tar dyes." Aniline dye stains are available today in three types, based on the solvent used to dissolve them. They are water stains, spirit stains, and non-grain-raising stains (Illus. 10-11).

Aniline Water Stain

Aniline water stain is an aniline dye stain that is soluble in water. It is considered the most permanent and offers the greatest clarity of all the aniline wood stains. Many different colors are available. Water stains will always leave the grain clear and visible, even if several coats of stain are used to deepen the color.

Although water stains have many advantages, they do have two major drawbacks. First, they will raise the grain, leaving the surface fuzzy with small wood fibres; second, the water can soften the glue used to secure veneers or cause the veneer to swell and buckle. When applying water to the wood surface will create problems, a spirit stain or a non-grain-raising stain should be used.

Water stains are sold in large cans to professional wood finishers, but for advanced amateurs the small packets that make a quart of stain are more convenient. These smaller

Water Stain	Spirit Stain	NGR Stain

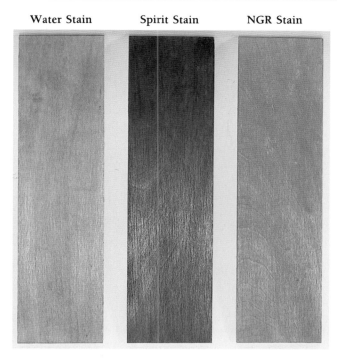

Illus. 10-11. Aniline dyes can produce a wide range of colors ranging from natural-looking wood tones to bright colors. There are three types of aniline stain. These maple samples have each been stained with a different type. The sample on the left was stained with water stain. The name of the color is Early-American maple. The sample in the middle was stained with walnut spirit stain. The sample on the right was stained with orange non-grain-raising stain.

quantities are sold through the mail-order woodworking catalogues.

To make the stain, boil one quart of water and pour it into a glass jar. Pour in the contents of the packet or one ounce of the bulk stain. Stir the stain thoroughly. After the stain has cooled, pour it through a cloth strainer to remove any undissolved particles. The liquid stain will keep indefinitely if you store it in a tightly sealed glass container. Don't use a metal can, because the stain will corrode the metal and the metal will discolor the stain.

Apply the stain with a brush or sponge. The modern foam brushes work very well. Apply the stain evenly, because lap marks and variations in color are hard to remedy. Unlike pigmented oil stains, you do not wipe the stain after application; the stain is left on the wood to soak deeply into the fibres.

You can get a more even application if you dilute the stain with water and apply several coats, allowing the stain

to dry between coats. You can also sand between coats when using this technique, to remove raised grain fibres. Each additional coat will deepen the color of the stain. It is easier to produce the exact color intensity desired through this method, because you can see the effect of each coat and stop when the correct intensity is achieved. If a single intense coat is applied, it is often darker than desired.

Aniline Spirit Stain

Aniline spirit stains are aniline dyes that dissolve in alcohol. They won't raise the grain and they don't swell the wood, so they are safer to use on veneers. Spirit stains dry quickly. This makes them slightly more difficult to apply, and they won't soak into the wood as deeply as a water stain.

Generally, a spirit stain has almost the same color as its corresponding water stain. Spirit stains are not as light-fast as water stains, but they are much more permanent than most of the natural stains. Spirit stains are often used for touch-up work. They are compatible with shellac, so they can be used to tint shellac.

To mix the stain, add the dry powder to alcohol and stir. Some types must first be dissolved in a small quantity of methyl alcohol (wood alcohol), and then the dissolved liquid can be mixed with ethyl alcohol (shellac thinner). Others can be dissolved directly in ethyl alcohol. Store the liquid stain in a brown-glass container away from sunlight.

Apply the stain carefully, because it dries so quickly that lap marks are a common problem.

Non-Grain-Raising Stain

A non-grain-raising stain combines the clarity and permanence of a water stain with the non-grain-raising capacity and fast drying times of a spirit stain. The name non-grain-raising stain is often abbreviated to NGR stain.

An NGR stain uses dyes similar to the ones used for water stains, but they are dissolved in a special mix of solvents. Glycol, acetone, toluol, and alcohol may be used in various combinations and proportions to make an NGR stain. The exact composition of the solvent is a trade secret of each manufacturer. The stains are only sold in liquid form.

NGR stain was developed mainly as an industrial stain for use in large furniture factories where it is applied with spray equipment. Spraying is the preferred method of application, because its fast drying time makes it difficult to apply with a brush. Some types of NGR stain contain a retarder that slows the drying process; these stains can be successfully applied with a brush.

CHAPTER ELEVEN

Chemical Stains and Fuming

WOOD CONTAINS NATURAL coloring materials. Many of the natural dyes are derived from wood. As described in Chapter Ten, when certain chemicals are combined with these natural dyes, a chemical change takes place that can alter the color of the dye.

The chemicals in chemical stains perform the same function as the mordants described in Chapter Ten. They combine with the natural colorants of the wood to alter the chemical composition of the wood and produce a different color. Woods that are high in natural-coloring materials such as tannin are particularly well suited for chemical staining, but some of the chemical stains will work on other woods as well.

Chemical stains can be very beautiful and natural-looking because they take emphasize the natural substances already in the wood. Variations in grain color can be maintained because the concentration of the chemicals in the wood will vary, depending on the grain structure. Chemical stains can be used to emphasize the grain pattern of wood; this is often very effective when working with fancy grains such as found on burls or bird's-eye wood.

Chemical stains are not as predictable as other types of stains, so it will always take some experimentation to achieve the desired results. The chemicals used can be hazardous, so use extreme caution when working with them. Always wear goggles and protective gloves and clothing. Work in a well-ventilated area, to avoid inhaling the fumes, and, if necessary, wear a respirator to prevent inhalation of toxic fumes. Observe all safety warnings that appear on the chemical containers.

The acids are particularly dangerous; I don't recommend that you use formulas that contain acid, unless you are familiar with the safety precautions and have had experience with handling acids. Most of the acids should be diluted before use. Take extreme care when diluting acids. *Never pour water into the acid.* This can result in a violent reaction that will spray acid all over. Instead, fill a container with the required amount of water and pour the acid into the water.

Many of the chemicals used come as dry powders or crystals. They must be dissolved in water before use.

Minerals in the water can cause unexpected colors to appear in the stain, so old formulas usually recommend using rainwater; you can use distilled water. Tap water may be alright, if it is low in mineral content. If you are considering using tap water, make up a test batch of the stain using your tap water and stain some samples of wood. If unexpected black or grey shades appear in the stain, then your water contains too much iron and you should use distilled water.

Some powders may not dissolve completely at first; if possible, make up the solutions well in advance and let the chemicals dissolve for several days. As a general rule, one gallon of chemical stain will treat about 600 square feet of wood surface.

Chemical stains can be applied with a sponge or a brush. Natural-bristle brushes will become limp and useless when used with chemical stains; the traditional type of brush used was made from tampico, a natural plant fibre that is resistant to chemicals. Today, you can use a synthetic-bristle brush such as one with nylon or polyester bristles.

Chemical stains will raise the grain of the wood, so you should dampen the wood and sand it as described in Chapter Two before you apply a chemical stain. If you allow a chemical stain to drip onto bare wood as you are brushing it onto another area, the drips will show. Even after you have applied the chemical over the area where the drips fell, the drips will still show up as darker spots. To avoid this problem, start at the bottom of the project and work towards the top; then accidental drips will fall on areas that have already been treated with the chemical. Now, if you brush out the drip or wipe it off with a rag as soon as it falls, the drip will not show.

CHEMICALS USED TO MAKE STAINS

Illus. 11-1 shows some of the commonly used chemicals. Illus. 11-2 shows how some chemicals react with different types of wood. The following sections describe most of the chemicals you will see in old formulas.

Tannic Acid

Tannic acid is one of the most basic ingredients in chem-

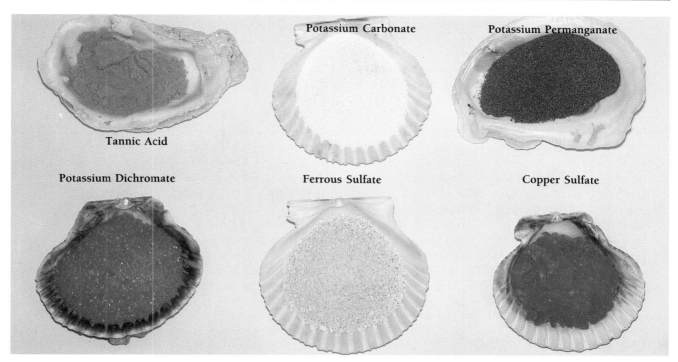

Illus. 11-1. Most of the chemicals used as wood stains come as dry powders or crystals. They must be dissolved in water before use. The chemicals shown in the top row, from left to right, are tannic acid, potassium carbonate, and potassium permanganate. On the bottom row, from left to right, are potassium dichromate, ferrous sulfate, and copper sulfate.

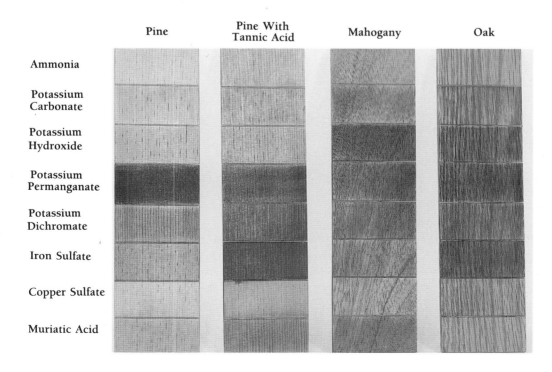

Illus. 11-2. These samples show the effects of some chemical stains on different types of wood. From left to right, the samples are pine, pine washed with tannic acid before other chemicals were applied, mahogany, and oak.

The chemicals used on these samples, from top to bottom, are ammonia, potassium carbonate, potassium hydroxide, potassium permanganate, potassium dichromate, ferrous sulfate, copper sulfate, and muriatic acid.

ical staining. It is a natural chemical that is found in many plants and in woods such as oak, walnut, and mahogany. Tannic acid will react with other chemicals to make a range of brown tones, greys, and blacks. When tannic acid is a naturally occurring chemical in the wood, it is called "tannin." In the past, tannin was extracted from plant materials that were high in tannin content. Oak galls were one of the primary sources. The oak galls were boiled in water, and the strained liquid was then applied to the wood. Today, pure tannic acid is commercially available.

Woods such as oak that have a high tannin content can be chemically stained without additional tannin. Woods that are low in tannin require an application of tannic acid before some of the chemical stains will be effective. To make a solution for this purpose, mix three teaspoons of tannic acid powder with 8 ounces of water. Apply the solution to the work and let it dry before applying any other chemicals.

Tannic acid is toxic if eaten or inhaled and has recently been suspected of being carcinogenic, so wear gloves and a filtre mask when working with concentrated tannic acid.

Ammonia

Ammonia reacts with tannin to produce a range of brown tones. Industrial-strength ammonia produces the best results, but household-strength ammonia can be used—in the fuming process or applied as a liquid. An important advantage ammonia has over other chemicals is that it completely evaporates from the wood. Other alkalies leave a residue that must be neutralized.

Concentrated ammonia fumes may be fatal; even in low concentrations, the fumes will irritate your eyes and nose. Use ammonia outside or in a well-ventilated area.

Potassium Carbonate

Potassium carbonate (or potash) is an alkali and produces brown tones similar to those produced by ammonia. It comes as a powder that must be dissolved in water before use. It leaves a residue on the wood after it has dried. To remove the residue, wash the wood with clean water; then neutralize the potassium carbonate by washing it with household vinegar. Finally, wash the wood with clean water again. Potassium carbonate is a skin irritant and poisonous.

Potassium Hydroxide

Potassium hydroxide is another strong alkali. It will produce darker browns than potassium carbonate or ammonia. It comes as a powder that must be dissolved in water before use. It leaves a residue on the wood after it has dried. To remove the residue, wash the wood with clean water, and then neutralize the potassium hydroxide by washing the wood with household vinegar. Finally, wash the wood with clean water again. It, too, is a skin irritant and poisonous.

Sodium Hydroxide

Sodium hydroxide (lye, or caustic soda) is another alkali and it is similar to the others in effect. Like potash, it must be neutralized by washing it away with water and vinegar. Like the above chemicals, it is irritating to the skin and poisonous.

Potassium Permanganate

Potassium permanganate (or permanganate of potash) is one of the more important of the chemical stains. It produces a wide range of beautiful browns when applied to high-tannin woods or over a wash of tannic acid. It comes in crystal form. To prepare a working solution for a medium brown color, dissolve ½ ounce of crystals into one quart of water. The solution will first turn the wood violet, but the violet color will change to brown as the wood dries. Potassium permanganate is caustic, so dilute it.

Potassium Dichromate

Potassium dichromate (or bichromate of potash) is similar to potassium permanganate in effect, but the color produced tends to be more yellowish. It is toxic if inhaled or eaten.

Iron Compounds

Iron compounds produce grey to black colors. Each coat will darken the color; after several coats, the color will be a deep black similar to ebony. A light wash can be used to give new wood the silver-grey color of weathered wood. The iron reacts with tannin, so woods low in tannin should be pre-treated with tannic acid before applying the iron compounds.

In the past, wood finishers frequently made their own iron stains by putting iron nails, scraps of steel, iron filings, or worn-out steel wool into a earthenware crock of vinegar. A loose-fitting lid was placed over the crock. It is important not to use a tightly sealed lid, because the chemical reaction releases a gas that can build up sufficient pressure to burst a sealed container. The iron was left in the vinegar for an extended time. It could be used after about a week, but the solution continued to get stronger the longer the iron remained in the vinegar. Before use, the solution was strained.

Wood finishers of the past often purchased ready-made

iron compounds, and these iron compounds are still available today. The ready-made compounds are more reliable than shop-made compounds and you can duplicate your results better because you have a known concentration of iron in the solution each time you mix up a batch of stain. One of the most commonly used iron compounds used was called "copperas" or "green copperas"; today, it is called iron sulfate or ferrous sulfate. Iron chloride is another commercially available iron compound.

Copper Sulfate

Copper sulfate is a copper compound that produces a grey-brown color when applied to wood. Ammonia applied after the copper sulfate will enhance the effect. Copper sulfate is called "bluestone," "blue copperas," or "blue vitriol" in old formulas.

Nitric Acid

Nitric acid is highly corrosive and should be used with great care. Use it in very diluted amounts. The fumes are toxic. Wear eye protection and protective gloves and clothing when using nitric acid. It stains wood a yellow color that ranges from reddish to brownish. It is called "aquafortis" in old formulas.

Sulfuric Acid

Sulfuric acid is the acid used in automobile batteries. Like nitric acid, great care should be exercised when working with this chemical, as it is toxic and irritating to the skin. When applied full-strength to pine, it makes a green stain. It will produce a weathered-grey effect on pine when a diluted solution is used. On woods containing tannin, it produces a yellow color when diluted and a deep brown color when used full-strength. It is often called "oil of vitriol" in old formulas. A very diluted solution of sulfuric acid is sometimes called "sour water" in old formulas.

Muriatic Acid

Muriatic acid is the industrial form of hydrochloric acid. It is another highly corrosive liquid that can cause serious injury if care is not taken when using it. Use it in a very diluted form. The fumes are toxic. It turns in woods high in tannin, such as oak, greyish brown. Woods low in tannin, such as pine, turn grey when treated with muriatic acid.

Copper Acetate

This greenish blue chemical is sometimes specified as a mordant in old formulas. It is poisonous, so be careful not to get it on your hands or in your mouth.

Alum

Alum (potassium aluminum sulfate) is used as a mordant with natural dye stains; it makes the stain more permanent. It doesn't have much effect on the color of wood that has not been stained with a natural dye.

Cream of Tartar

Cream of tartar (potassium bitartrate) is sometimes used as a mordant with natural dye stains. It is used in cooking and can be purchased at a grocery store.

Glauber's Salt

Glauber's salt (sodium sulfate) is sometimes called for in old formulas as a mordant.

Pyrogallic Acid

Pyrogallic acid (pyrogallol) can be used instead of tannic acid to pretreat wood before applying other chemicals, as, for example, to pre-treat wood before fuming or applying liquid ammonia.

Tin Chloride

Tin chloride (stannous chloride) has been used as a mordant for over 5,000 years. Old formulas call it "tin crystals."

Vinegar

Vinegar (acetic acid) is used to neutralize alkali solutions. It can also be used to make an iron stain. (See Iron Compounds.)

Oxalic Acid

Oxalic acid will bleach the color from wood. It is poisonous, so wear gloves and protective goggles and avoid inhaling it or getting it in your mouth.

CHEMICAL STAIN FORMULAS

The following formulas are based on traditional formulas used throughout the classic era of wood finishing. You will have to experiment with the concentrations of the ingredients in these formulas to achieve the desired effect on the particular wood you are staining. These formulas will give you a starting point for developing the correct proportions for the stains.

Chemical stains offer a wide variation in color, depending on the strength of the solution used and the chemicals chosen, so you have many options available during the staining process. But, you will need to experiment before deciding on the final formula. Measure the amount accurately using a scale and graduated flask, and keep a record of your experiments so that you can duplicate your formulas at a later time. Mix chemicals in glass or earthenware containers. Don't use metal containers, because the chemicals can react with the metal to produce unexpected colors.

CHEMICAL STAIN #1 (ILLUS. 11-3)

Color: Brown

Woods It Is Effective On: oak, walnut, chestnut, and mahogany

Chemicals Used: ammonia

Brush or sponge the ammonia onto the wood. Let it dry. Repeat applications until the color desired is achieved.

Illus. 11-3. Ammonia stains. Left, oak stained with ammonia. Right, pine with a wash of tannic acid, followed with ammonia.

CHEMICAL STAIN #2 (ILLUS. 11-3)

Color: Light brown

Woods It Is Effective On: birch, maple, pine, and fir

Chemicals Used: tannic acid and ammonia

Mix three teaspoons of powdered tannic acid with 8 ounces of water. Apply the solution to the wood. Let it dry, and then apply the ammonia.

CHEMICAL STAIN #3 (ILLUS. 11-4)

Color: Honey-pine

Woods It Is Effective On: birch, maple, pine, and fir

Chemicals Used: tannic acid and potassium hydroxide

Mix three teaspoons of powdered tannic acid with 8 ounces of water. Apply the solution to the wood and let it dry. Mix one teaspoon of potassium-hydroxide crystals with 8 ounces of water. Apply the potassium-hydroxide solution to the wood.

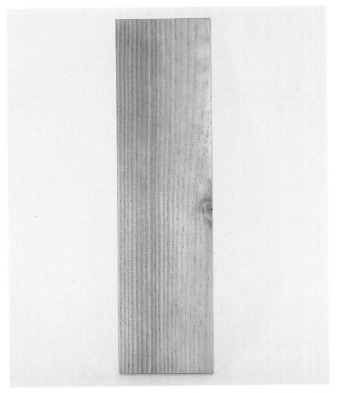

Illus. 11-4. Pine with a wash of tannic acid, followed with potassium hydroxide.

CHEMICAL STAIN #4 (ILLUS. 11-5)

Color: Yellowish brown

Woods It Is Effective On: oak, mahogany, cherry, walnut, and chestnut

Chemicals Used: potassium dichromate and vinegar

This stain will enhance the color of mahogany and give the grain added depth. It was used in France to treat Cuban mahogany during the Empire period. It will also produce warm browns on other high-tannin woods.

Mix one ounce of potassium dichromate in one quart of hot water (about 130 degrees Fahrenheit). Apply the potassium-dichromate solution to the wood, and then let the wood dry. Apply more stain if a darker color is desired. Neutralize the solution by washing the wood with clean water, and then washing it with vinegar. Finally, wash off the vinegar.

CHEMICAL STAIN #5 (ILLUS. 11-5)

Color: Yellowish brown

Woods It Is Effective On: birch, maple, pine, and fir

Chemicals Used: tannic acid, potassium dichromate, and vinegar

Mix three teaspoons of powdered tannic acid with 8 ounces of water. Apply the solution to the wood and let it dry. Mix one ounce of potassium dichromate in one quart of hot water (about 130 degrees Fahrenheit). Apply this solution to the wood. Let the wood dry. Neutralize the solution by washing the wood with clean water, followed by a wash with vinegar. Finally, wash off the vinegar.

CHEMICAL STAIN #6 (ILLUS. 11-6)

Color: Dark brown

Woods It Is Effective On: walnut, gum, and oak

Chemicals Used: potassium permanganate and vinegar

Dissolve one ounce of potassium permanganate in one quart of water. Apply the solution to the wood and let it dry. Sand off any raised grain and repeat the application of chemicals. Repeated applications of the potassium permanganate solution will darken the color. Let the wood dry. Neutralize the solution by washing the wood with clean water, followed by a wash with vinegar. Finally, wash off the vinegar.

CHEMICAL STAIN #7 (ILLUS. 11-6)

Color: Dark brown to black

Woods It Is Effective On: walnut and gum

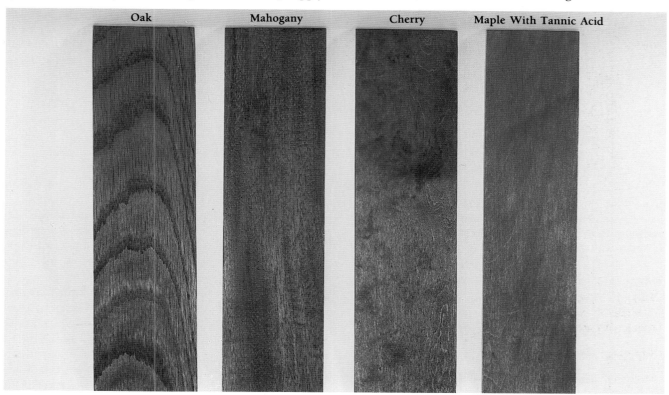

Illus. 11-5. Potassium-dichromate stains. From left to right are oak, mahogany, cherry, and maple treated with tannic acid before the potassium dichromate is applied.

Chemicals Used: potassium permanganate and iron sulfate

Dissolve one ounce of potassium permanganate in one quart of water. Brush the solution onto the wood and let it dry. Dissolve one ounce of iron sulfate in water; apply the iron-sulfate solution to the wood after the potassium-permanganate solution has completely dried. Let the wood dry, and then wash it with clean water.

Illus. 11-6. Potassium permanganate stains. At left, oak stained with potassium permanganate. At right is walnut stained with potassium permanganate, followed with ferrous sulfate.

CHEMICAL STAIN #8 (ILLUS. 11-7)

Color: Greyish brown

Woods It Is Effective On: mahogany

Chemical Used: iron sulfate

Dissolve one ounce of iron sulfate in water and apply the solution to mahogany wood. It will change the reddish tone of the wood to a greyish brown color. Test the solution's effect on a scrap of the same species of wood. If the wood has a bluish tint after you have applied the stain, then dilute the stain and test it again until the correct color is achieved.

CHEMICAL STAIN #9 (ILLUS. 11-7)

Color: Ebony-black

Woods It Is Effective On: oak and walnut

Chemical Used: iron sulfate

Dissolve one ounce of iron sulfate in one quart of water. Apply repeated coats of the solution to the wood until a dark grey-black color is produced. Wash the wood with clean water. After a finish is applied, the wood will be deep black in color.

CHEMICAL STAIN #10 (ILLUS. 11-7)

Color: Weathered grey

Woods It Is Effective On: pine and fir

Chemicals Used: tannic acid and iron sulfate

Mix three teaspoons of powdered tannic acid with 8 ounces of water. Apply the solution to the wood and let it dry. Dissolve one ounce of iron sulfate in a quart of water. When the tannic-acid solution is dry, apply the solution of iron sulfate. Wash the wood with clean water. For a weathered-grey color, don't apply any additional finish. If you apply oil or varnish, the color will loose its silver-grey quality and appear blacker.

CHEMICAL BLEACHING

Sunlight changes the natural colors of wood. Softwoods such as pine darken after long exposure to sunlight. Dark hardwoods such as walnut will get lighter after long exposure to sunlight. This sun-bleached effect is seen on many antiques.

Chemical bleaches can be used to simulate the effect of sun-bleaching. This can be useful if you are trying to match a repaired section to the rest of an antique, or if you are making a reproduction and you want its color to be the same as a sun-bleached original.

If you want to prevent sun-bleaching from eventually lightening the color of a dark wood, apply a lightfast stain to the wood. If you use a stain that closely matches the natural color of the wood, the effect will be hardly noticeable at first; but, when compared to an unstained sample years later, the stained wood will retain the original color while the unstained sample has become much lighter (Illus. 11-8).

Oxalic acid was one chemical used in bleaches by old-time wood finishers. It is available as crystals that must be dissolved in water before use. Dissolve four ounces of oxalic-acid crystals in one quart of hot water. Apply the solution to the wood while it is hot and let it dry; then neutralize it by washing the wood with a solution of one ounce of borax in one quart of water. Follow that with a wash of clear water.

The best old formulas used two separate solutions that are mixed just before use or applied to the wood separately. The two solutions react with each other and the coloring material in the wood to bleach out the color. Modern two-part bleaches are still based on this chemistry.

You can buy two-part bleaches at most stores that sell finishing supplies. Wear goggles and protective gloves and clothing when you are working with bleaches. Follow the directions that come with the bleach. Generally, you apply the first solution and let it soak in, and then apply the second solution. After letting the second solution dry overnight, you must thoroughly wash off the wood. The instruction on some types of bleach recommend that another chemical be applied, to neutralize the chemicals that remain from the bleach.

Bleaching will raise the grain, so a light sanding is necessary after the wood is dry. Don't sand too hard, because the bleached effect is only on a thin layer at the surface. It is possible to sand through the bleached wood to darker wood below. After bleaching, you can apply a clear finish or stain the wood with a light-colored stain.

FUMING

All of the chemical processes described so far involve putting large quantities of water-based solutions on the wood. This will raise the grain and can lead to other problems such as swelling, buckling veneers, and loosened glued joints. The fuming process uses ammonia fumes to darken woods that are high in tannin. It won't raise the grain or cause the other problems associated with water on wood, because only the chemical fumes touch the wood. It also produces a very even application of the chemical, even on very intricate pieces, and it can be used to treat all surfaces of assembled furniture.

Ammonia fumes are so penetrating that they will even penetrate below some finishes such as shellac and darken the wood. This property can be used to an advantage if you are not satisfied with the color of a piece after the

Illus. 11-7. Ferrous-sulfate stains. From left to right are mahogany, oak, and pine treated with tannic acid and then coated with ferrous sulfate.

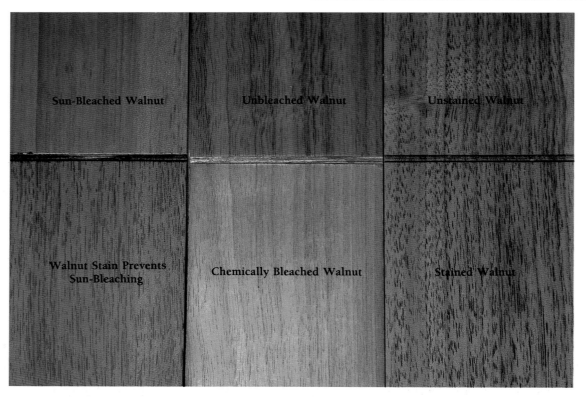

Illus. 11-8. This set of samples shows the effect of sun and chemical bleaching on walnut. All of the samples in the top row are simply sealed with a clear finish. The sample on the far left of the top row has been exposed to sunlight for several years. Notice the lightening effect the sun has had on the wood. This can be detected by comparing it to the unbleached walnut to the right of it and the unstained walnut on the far right. The sample directly below it has been exposed to the sun for the same length of time, but the wood was stained with a walnut stain before the clear finish was applied. Notice that the sample retains the original color of the wood.

The sample on the far right of the bottom row has also been stained; notice that it is difficult to tell any difference between the stained sample on the bottom row and the unstained sample directly above it. This shows that the staining doesn't alter the look of the wood initially, but it does protects the wood from sun-bleaching.

The sample in the middle of the bottom row has been chemically bleached to simulate the effects of extreme sun-bleaching. This technique is useful when you want to simulate the look of a very old sun-bleached antique.

finish is complete. You can darken the color through fuming. But generally, fuming is done before any other finishing steps.

Oak is the wood that is most often fumed. Fumed oak will range in color from light yellowish tan to dark brown; a medium brown is most common. The term "fumed oak" has even been applied to describe the color, and several stain formulas are listed in old sources that try to duplicate the color of fumed oak, but the best way to get a fumed-oak finish is to actually fume the wood with ammonia.

Other woods such as mahogany and chestnut can also be fumed.

The success of the fuming process depends on the tannin content of the wood, and even the tannin of woods with a high content can vary from one board to another. To make sure that the wood you are using can be fumed, brush some liquid ammonia on a scrap of the wood. If it darkens to the color you desire, then the wood can be fumed.

Woods that are low in tannin can be fumed if a wash

of tannic acid is applied first, but this step defeats the main advantage of fuming, because you now have to deal with the raised grain and other effects caused by applying a water solution to the wood. If you must apply a tannic acid wash, you might as well just brush on liquid ammonia instead of going through the trouble of making a fuming chamber.

In the past, fuming sizable pieces of furniture was usually limited to pieces made in large shops or factories, because an airtight fuming chamber was needed. This was a specially built room with a tightly sealed door. Today, we have the advantage of having lightweight plastic sheeting available to make a temporary fuming chamber large enough for any project (Illus. 11-9).

Illus. 11-9 (right). You will need an airtight fuming chamber to give a project a fumed oak finish. You can make a fuming tent by building a framework from 1 × 2 lumber and covering it with plastic sheeting. (Clear plastic lets you see how the color is progressing; but, if the project will receive direct sunlight, also cover the tent with an opaque tarp.) Spread out the plastic sheeting on the ground and place the furniture in the middle. Place the supporting framework over the piece of furniture. Place wide-mouthed jars full of ammonia inside the tent. Seal the tent closed with tape. The fumes will penetrate and color the entire surface of the furniture.

The ammonia fumes are irritating and can be toxic in large concentrations, so work outside or in a well-ventilated shed away from occupied buildings. Wear a respirator and goggles when you are working with ammonia. Remove all metal hardware from the furniture, because the am-

Illus. 11-10. This sample shows fumed oak with a black wax finish. This is a traditional way to finish fumed oak. The black wax emphasizes the pore pattern of the oak.

monia can react with the metal to make a black stain on the wood around the metal.

To construct a fuming chamber, you simply make a tent of plastic. The thin, clear-plastic tarps sold at paint stores work well. Make a framework of 1 × 2 lumber to support the tent. Spread out the plastic tarp on the ground and place the piece of furniture in the middle. Place the supporting framework over the piece of furniture. Loose parts such as doors can be leaned against the framework or the back of the project. If they just touch at a small corner, the fumes will penetrate and color the entire surface.

Now, place several wide-mouthed jars inside the tent and fill them with ammonia. Industrial-strength ammonia is better, but you can use household-strength; you will just need to use more of it.

Pull up the tarp and cover the framework completely.

Seal the tent with tape. If you are working outside or near a window, cover the tent with an opaque tarp. Sunlight can affect the fuming process, causing some areas to be darker than others.

The color will gradually darken over a period of hours. For the darkest shades, it will take about 24 hours. You can easily check on the progress, because the clear plastic allows you to clearly see the effects of the fuming. When the color is as dark as you want it, open the tent and let the wood air out.

Any finish can be applied over fumed wood. A traditional top coat is a thin coat of shellac followed with several coats of black or dark brown wax (Illus. 11-10). The wax fills the open pores of the oak and accentuates them. (See Chapter Nine.)

CHAPTER TWELVE

Milk Paint

WHEN A RURAL craftsman needed a durable and inexpensive wood finish, milk paint was often the first choice. The main ingredients in milk paint are milk, lime, and earth pigments. These ingredients were inexpensive and readily available to the craftsman from local sources. White milk paint was the easiest to make, because whiting was the only pigment needed, but colored milk paint was often made using locally available earth pigments.

Milk paint has a distinctive look that cannot be easily duplicated with other types of paint. The pigments and the lime are coarsely ground. This coarseness is revealed when the paint dries; the surface is slightly rough. The paint can be smoothed with abrasives or by years of wear, but even when the surface of the paint is worn very smooth, the coarse-grain structure of the paint is still discernible upon close examination.

The pigments used were natural earth colors, so they are more subdued than some of the bright color pigments used today. After exposure to sunlight for a long time, some of the pigments fade or change color. This can result in subtle mottling of the color as individual grains of pigment change differently. The result is often more beautiful than the original unfaded color.

Milk paint is very durable, as anyone who has tried to strip it off an old piece of furniture can affirm. The reason is a substance found in milk called "casein." Casein has been used for centuries as a glue and paint binder. It can be extracted from the milk, and, in its pure form, it is used to make casein paint and glue. In milk paint, the casein is not separated from the milk. This results in a slightly lower-quality paint than paint made with pure casein, but the ease old-time wood finishers had in making milk paint outweighed any disadvantages. The reason for using milk paint on a project today is to duplicate the distinctive look of the old pieces that were painted with it (Illus. 12-1).

You can buy dry powdered milk paint that uses traditional pigments (Illus. 12-2). This is probably the best way to get milk paint for your projects. The earth pigments used are authentic and have the correct coarse texture.

Finding appropriate pigments can be the hardest part of trying to make your own milk paint.

To prepare the dry-powder milk paint, mix the paint in an earthenware or glass container; don't use a metallic container, because the metal can react with the paint and cause discoloration. Enamelled metalware can be used if the enamelled surface is not broken.

Add water as directed in the instructions on the bag, and stir it thoroughly. You can use a wooden stick to stir the paint. A quick way to ensure thorough mixing is to use a paint stirrer that mounts in an electric drill.

After the paint is thoroughly mixed, it is usually advisable to strain it through several layers of cheesecloth. This will remove any large lumps of pigments (Illus. 12-3). If you want a really rough surface, it is okay to use the paint unstrained.

Mix only the amount you will use in one day. If you have some left over, it will keep overnight if placed in the

Illus. 12-1. This hanging shelf based on a Shaker design is finished with barn-red milk paint.

Illus. 12-2. Commercially available powdered milk paint is probably the best way for you to get a small quantity of authentic-looking milk paint. The powder comes in a sealed packet; once the seal is broken, the powder should be kept in a sealed jar or earthenware container that has an airtight seal.

Illus. 12-3. Milk paint will usually have some small lumps in it. If you want a very rough texture, it is okay to leave the lumps in the paint. If you want a smoother finish, strain the paint before use.

refrigerator, but the milk will soon go sour if you try to keep the mixed paint longer than two days. Any unused powdered-milk paint should be kept in a sealed glass jar or earthenware container to protect it from moisture. The powder will keep a long time if it is kept away from humid air. Moisture in the air will react with the lime. If the powder absorbs too much moisture, the paint won't harden properly after it is mixed and applied.

Making your own milk paint is not particularly difficult,

but it may be difficult to find appropriate pigments to color it. If you want white paint, all you need is some skim milk, whiting, and some slaked lime. See Illus. 12-4 for one traditional formula from the 1870 edition of William Dick's *Encyclopedia of Practical Receipts and Processes* (Illus. 12-4). Slaked lime is available at most lumberyards. It is an ingredient used in making brick mortar. Make sure that you get *slaked* lime. This is lime that has been hydrated by soaking it in water and then letting it dry. Quicklime is not hydrated; if you use it to make milk paint, the lime will react with the water and heat up. Whiting is fine-powdered chalk. It is a white pigment.

You can color the milk paint by adding colored pigments. Use dry-powder pigments that don't have any type of binder added. Some pigments will react with lime and change color or fade, so try a small sample batch first to make sure that the pigments will work. Most earth colors that are derived from natural minerals will work with milk paint.

APPLYING MILK PAINT

Apply milk paint with an inexpensive brush, because milk paint is hard on brushes. A nylon brush can be used; also, the disposable foam-type brushes work well. Milk paint can also be wiped on with a sponge or rag. This results in a thin coat that is more like a stain than a coat of paint.

There are several ways that you can apply milk paint. I will describe six methods. The method you choose depends on how you want the finished project to look. If you want the project to have a dull, rough surface, apply

---

2770. To Make Paint without Oil or Lead. Whiting, 5 pounds; skimmed milk, 2 quarts; fresh slacked lime, 2 ounces. Put the lime into a stone-ware vessel, pour upon it a sufficient quantity of the milk to make a mixture resembling cream; the balance of the milk is then to be added; and lastly the whiting is to be crumbled upon the surface of the fluid, in which it gradually sinks. At this period it must be well stirred in, or ground as you would other paint, and it is fit for use. There may be added any coloring matter that suits the fancy, to be applied in the same manner as other paints, and in a few hours it will become perfectly dry. Another coat may then be added, and so on until the work is done. This paint is of great tenacity, bears rubbing with a coarse cloth, has little smell, even when wet, and when dry is inodorous. It also possesses the merit of cheapness, the above quantity being sufficient for 57 yards.

Illus. 12-4. This excerpt from the *Encyclopedia of Practical Receipts and Processes* by William Dick gives a formula for making milk paint that was used in the 1870's.

the paint using the first method. This is the technique used originally for farm equipment and other rough pieces that needed the protection of paint but weren't intended as fine furniture.

The second method produces a smooth finish that is appropriate for furniture that was used in the house. The third method approximates the look of milk paint that has been worn through years of use. The fourth method uses oil to protect the paint and accentuate the color. The fifth method makes the project look as if it has been repainted several times during its history and has received hard use. The sixth method uses milk paint as a thin stain. This approximates the look of old milk paint that has been stripped off or worn away, leaving behind only the pigments that have soaked into the wood.

Method One
This is the way milk paint was originally applied to many

Illus. 12-5. These samples show how milk paint looks when it is applied without sanding between coats or smoothing with steel wool. This rough texture looks good on rustic projects.

pieces of farm equipment and large surfaces such as barn walls. It leaves the surface looking dull and rough. It will approximate the look of milk paint used on rustic pieces (Illus. 12-5).

Apply the paint with a brush in a thick coat. Let the paint dry for about one hour or until the color changes from the darker, wet look to the dull, dry look; then apply another coat of paint.

After the paint is dry, wipe it with a cloth or brush over it with a dry brush to remove any loose particles of paint.

Method Two

This is the method used to produce a smooth finish appropriate for furniture that was intended for use in the house.

The project should be prepared by smoothing the wood with planes and scrapers as described in Chapter Two. Before applying the paint, wet the wood with a dampened sponge or cloth (Illus. 12-6). This will help to keep the absorption of the paint even. Apply a coat of paint evenly over the surface and let it dry (Illus. 12-7). When the first coat is dry, it will look terrible; it will be splotchy and uneven, but don't worry, the second coat will even it all out and give a uniform finish.

Smooth the first coat by rubbing it with #00 steel wool or fine sandpaper (Illus. 12-8). A synthetic finishing pad is a modern substitute for steel wool. It works very well for this purpose and will last longer than steel wool.

Next, apply another coat of paint. When this coat is dry, smooth it with #0000 steel wool. Finally, buff the surface with a clean, dry cloth. The result will be a smooth finish with no gloss (Illus. 12-9).

Illus. 12-7. Applying the first coat of milk paint with a foam brush. You can use any type of inexpensive brush to apply milk paint.

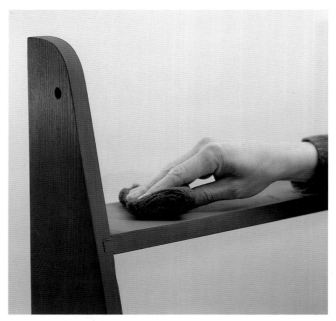

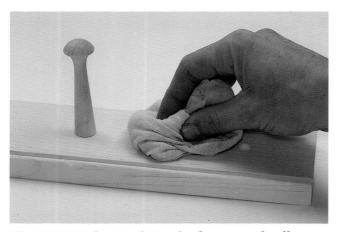

Illus. 12-6. Before applying the first coat of milk paint, wet the wood with a damp cloth. This will make it easier to apply an even coat of paint.

Illus. 12-8. Smooth the paint with #00 steel wool between coats. Buff the final coat with #0000 steel wool.

Illus. 12-9. After it has been buffed
with steel wool, the paint will be
smooth, but it won't have any gloss.

Method Three

This method is intended to approximate the look of a milk-paint finish that has been worn through years of use (Illus. 12-10).

Prepare the wood by smoothing it with planes and scrapers, and then sand it with 150-grit sandpaper (Illus.

12-11). As you sand, concentrate on areas that would normally receive a lot of wear, such as sharp corners and arrises. Round over the corners and arrises to simulate years of wear.

Apply the paint following the directions given in Method Two (Illus. 12-12), but when you smooth the paint

Illus. 12-10. The milk paint on this
table looks as if it has had many
years of wear. This timeworn effect
looks good on antique reproductions.

Illus. 12-11. To give a project a time-worn finish, start by sanding it smooth and rounding the corners and arrises.

Illus. 12-14 shows samples of milk paint with oil; the red and green samples have oil on their bottom halves. Their top halves show the color of the paint without oil. Notice how the application of oil has enhanced the color and added a satin gloss to the paint while still maintaining the characteristic look of milk paint.

Apply the paint following the directions given in Method Two. After the final coat of paint has dried and you have smoothed it with steel wool, wipe the surface with a rag dampened with linseed oil. The oil will soak into the paint and bring out the color. The oil will also give the paint a satin gloss and make it more water-resistant.

You can substitute a modern oil finish instead of linseed oil, if you want. The modern oils such as tung oil or Danish oil will dry faster and give the paint a harder surface. One of the advantages of using the more authentic linseed oil is that that oil will darken over time. This is characteristic of old paint. The darkened linseed oil adds character to the color.

You can simulate this darkening effect by using a tinted oil. (See Chapter Eight.) Use a medium brown color to tint the oil. When you apply the oil, it will darken the color of the pigments in the paint and warm the color. The result approximates the look of paint that has aged for many years. The pumpkin and blue samples in Illus. 12-14 have been given a coat of tinted oil on their lower halves. Their upper halves have a coat of clear oil.

Illus. 12-12. Give the project at least two coats of paint following the instructions given for Method Two.

with the steel wool or sandpaper, sand through the paint to bare wood at the arrises and other high spots or areas that would receive a lot of wear (Illus. 12-13).

Method Four

With this method, an application of oil is used to produce a smooth finish that has a satin gloss. The oil will enhance the color of the paint and protect the paint from moisture. It can be used in conjunction with any of the other methods described. It is very appropriate for furniture. It will approximate the look of the paint used on Windsor chairs.

Illus. 12-13. After the final coat is dry, rub the paint with steel wool. Rub through to bare wood in areas such as corners and arrises that would naturally receive a lot of wear.

Illus. 12-14. After the final coat is dry and has been smoothed with steel wool, you can apply a coat of oil to protect the paint and accentuate the color. The red and green samples on the left have oil on their lower halves. Their upper halves have no oil. Notice how the oil darkens the color and gives the paint a satin gloss. The pumpkin and blue samples on the right illustrate how tinted oil can give the paint an aged look. These samples have clear oil on their upper halves and brown-tinted oil on their lower halves.

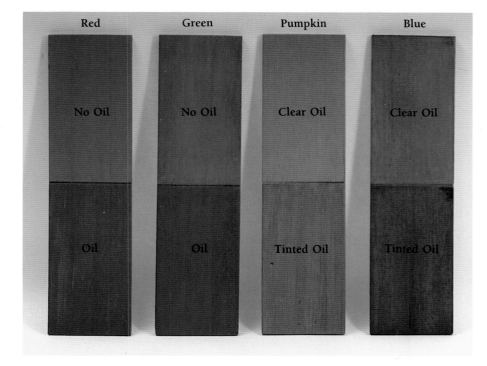

Method Five

I call this method "giving the piece a history." It approximates the look of a piece that has received several coats of paint over the years that have, through wear, been exposed (Illus. 12-15).

Apply the paint following the directions given in Method Two. Choose at least two contrasting colors of paint. In this example, I used red for the first coat (Illus. 12-16). Let the first coat dry, and smooth it as described above; then apply a different color of paint for the second

Illus. 12-15. I have given this chest a "history" by first applying a coat of red paint and then switching to green paint for the second coat. Distressing and sanding exposed areas of red paint gives the chest the look of an antique that has had several coats of paint and a lot of wear.

Illus. 12-16. First, apply a coat of paint following the directions given for Method Two. When the first coat of paint is dry, apply a second coat using a different color of paint.

coat. I used green for the second coat. I stopped at two coats, but you can use as many as you like, changing colors for each coat.

After the final coat is dry, distress the finish by hitting it with various objects such a piece of chain or tools that you drop on the surface. This will chip off some of the paint, exposing different colors beneath; then smooth the surface with steel wool. Rub through to bare wood at the arrises and other areas of high wear. In other areas, rub through to underlying layers of paint (Illus. 12-17). You can apply oil to the finish or simply burnish the paint by rubbing it hard with a soft cloth.

Method Six

With this method, milk paint is used like a stain to color the wood, but the grain will be allowed to show through. It approximates the look of an antique that was painted at one time, but the paint has either worn off or has been stripped. All that is left of the original paint film is the pigment that has soaked into the pores of the wood.

Thin the paint by adding water, and then apply it with a brush or rag (Illus. 12-18). Let it soak into the wood for a few minutes, but don't let it dry. Now, wipe the paint off with another rag. If the paint won't wipe off as much as you want, wet the rag with water and wash off the paint. If the resulting coat is too light, you can apply another coat after the first coat is dry.

Let the paint dry, and then smooth the surface with steel wool or sandpaper. You can apply any clear finish on top of the stain. Oil looks good, or you can apply a clear varnish.

Illus. 12-17. You can see in this close-up how the red paint shows through the green after the paint has been sanded.

Illus. 12-18. Milk paint thinned with water can be used to stain wood. Apply the thinned paint with a brush or rag and then wipe most of it off. This leaves just the pigments that have soaked into the wood. The milk paint stain makes the project look like an old piece that was originally painted and then had its paint removed.

Bibliography

THIS SECTION CONTAINS a list and descriptions of the old wood-finishing books and other materials I have found to be useful during 18 years of research on wood finishing.

1. Dick, William. *Encyclopedia of Practical Receipts and Processes*. New York, 1875.

This book contains over 6,400 recipes and formulas for all types of industrial and domestic products used in the 1870's. Apparently, Dick used information from other books of the period to compile this encyclopedia. He used virtually all of the information in *The Cabinet-Maker's Guide,* and there are other wood-finishing formulas from other sources. Unfortunately, Dick didn't credit his sources, so it is difficult to tell where his formulas came from.

This book has been reprinted, so you should be able to find a copy.

2. Roubo, André Jacques. *L'Art du Menuisier en Meubles* (The Art of the Woodworker). Paris, 1769.

This is a very important book for those who are researching all aspects of woodworking in the 1700's. Unfortunately for English-speaking researchers, it is written in French. Original copies of this book are very rare. It is available on microfiche.

3. Sheraton, Thomas. *The Cabinet Dictionary*. London, 1803.

Thomas Sheraton was the author of the influential work *The Cabinet-Maker and Upholsterer's Drawing Book*. In *The Cabinet Dictionary,* he explains the terms used in cabinetmaking, chair-making, and upholstery. The book is arranged as a dictionary, with the terms in alphabetical order. There are several useful entries regarding varnish-making and polishing.

4. Stalker, John, and George Parker. *A Treatise of Japaning and Varnishing*. Oxford, 1688.

This is probably one of the very first do-it-yourself books. In the late 1600's, trade between Japan and Europe was opening up. Europeans were very interested in Japanese products, and Japanese-style furniture was very fashionable. This book was written for ladies and gentlemen who wanted to decorate furniture with Japanese scenes as a hobby. It is very useful because it gives details about many of the finishing materials available in the late 1600's.

5. *The Cabinet-Maker's Guide* ... Greenfield, Massachusetts: Ansel Phelps, 1825.

It is unfortunate that the author's name was not included in this book. This anonymous wood finisher has made a great contribution to our knowledge of early 19th-century wood-finishing techniques. Ansel Phelps is listed as the publisher of the 1825 edition and Jacob B. Moore is listed as the printer of the 1827 edition. The information in these two editions is identical.

The Cabinet-Maker's Guide is a very rare book. There are probably fewer than 15 copies of the 1825 and 1827 editions in libraries and private collections. I am grateful to the Smithsonian Institution Library for allowing me to use the copy they have. Fortunately, most of the formulas from *The Cabinet-Maker's Guide* were included in William Dick's *Encyclopedia of Practical Receipts and Processes,* which has been reprinted.

6. *The Story of Shellac*. Somerset, New Jersey: William Zinsser & Co., Inc., 1989.

This is an interesting pamphlet produced by the manufacturer of Bulls Eye Shellac. It details the process of harvesting and refining shellac. Some of the material is reprinted from a pamphlet the company produced in 1913.

7. *A.F. Suter Data Sheets*. London: A.F. Suter & Co., Ltd.

A.F. Suter is the manufacturer of Swanlac products. They market a complete line of seed-lacs, shellacs, natural resins, and waxes. They provided me with a set of data sheets that detail the physical and chemical properties of their products.

METRIC SYSTEM

Unit	Abbreviation	Approximate U.S. Equivalent		
Length				
		Number of Metres		
myriametre	mym	10,000	6.2 miles	
kilometre	km	1000	0.62 mile	
hectometre	hm	100	109.36 yards	
dekametre	dam	10	32.81 feet	
metre	m	1	39.37 inches	
decimetre	dm	0.1	3.94 inches	
centimetre	cm	0.01	0.39 inch	
millimetre	mm	0.001	0.04 inch	
Area				
		Number of Square Metres		
square kilometre	sq km *or* km^2	1,000,000	0.3861 square miles	
hectare	ha	10,000	2.47 acres	
are	a	100	119.60 square yards	
centare	ca	1	10.76 square feet	
square centimetre	sq cm *or* cm^2	0.0001	0.155 square inch	
Volume				
		Number of Cubic Metres		
dekastere	das	10	13.10 cubic yards	
stere	s	1	1.31 cubic yards	
decistere	ds	0.10	3.53 cubic feet	
cubic centimetre	cu cm *or* cm^3 *also* cc	0.000001	0.061 cubic inch	
Capacity				
		Number of Litres	*Cubic*	*Dry*	*Liquid*

Unit	Abbreviation	*Number of Litres*	*Cubic*	*Dry*	*Liquid*
kilolitre	kl	1000	1.31 cubic yards		
hectolitre	hl	100	3.53 cubic feet	2.84 bushels	
dekalitre	dal	10	0.35 cubic foot	1.14 pecks	2.64 gallons
litre	l	1	61.02 cubic inches	0.908 quart	1.057 quarts
decilitre	dl	0.10	6.1 cubic inches	0.18 pint	0.21 pint
centilitre	cl	0.01	0.6 cubic inch		0.338 fluidounce
millilitre	ml	0.001	0.06 cubic inch		0.27 fluidram

Unit	Abbreviation	*Number of Grams*	Approximate U.S. Equivalent
Mass and Weight			
metric ton	MT *or* t	1,000,000	1.1 tons
quintal	q	100,000	220.46 pounds
kilogram	kg	1,000	2.2046 pounds
hectogram	hg	100	3.527 ounces
dekagram	dag	10	0.353 ounce
gram	g *or* gm	1	0.035 ounce
decigram	dg	0.10	1.543 grains
centigram	cg	0.01	0.154 grain
milligram	mg	0.001	0.015 grain

Index

127